ENDORSEMENTS

Suffering is a universal experience as my good friend, Cindy Brinker Simmons, states in her stirring book, *Restored: Reconnecting Life's Broken Pieces*. Life is hard. Crisis and adversity crash into all our lives eventually. Cindy's relentless joy and impassioned writing, combined with her vibrant faith, masterfully reiterate one unwavering truth: hope is found in trusting God. I encourage you to read *Restored*. It will inspire you!

—*Norm Miller,* chairman emeritus, Interstate Batteries

Are you in pain? Devastated by heartbreak and loss, suffering a broken body or a broken relationship? Cindy Brinker Simmons has been right where you are. She has asked every wrenching, honest question that plagues you. The book you are holding is a gift. It is an invitation to put yourself into the hands of a compassionate, wise, trustworthy companion along the journey toward hope, toward a healing you may not yet imagine. Each tender story, bold insight, and practical application is hard won, born of Cindy's life, experienced wholly, deeply, faithfully. Invite Cindy to walk with you now, as she shows the way into restoration and true joy. Seriously Love. This. Book.

—*Karen Marsh,* executive director,
Theological Horizons at the University of Virginia

Few of us have endured the personal pain that has stamped Cindy Brinker Simmons's life, and even fewer of us have learned to turn it into joy. With a unique empathy, a remarkable warmth, and an absolute conviction in her faith, she leads us on a journey of discovery—a discovery of how to find light in darkness, how to find hope when all may seem lost. She speaks with the authority of authenticity, and that's a rare quality.

—*Stephen Galloway,* dean of Chapman University's Dodge College
of Film and Media Arts; former executive editor of
The Hollywood Reporter; *New York Times* best-selling author

In *Restored,* Cindy Brinker Simmons bravely shares her personal life stories. In her words and reference to Scripture, the Bible comes alive. She provides such valuable tools and guidance to the reader to deal with life's many challenges. After reading *Restored,* I was filled with joy and hopefulness—two things we all need more of in life.

—*Marianne Staubach,* beloved wife of Hall of Famer
and legendary Dallas Cowboys quarterback Roger Staubach;
devoted mother, grandmother, and great-grandmother

My dear friend, Cindy Brinker Simmons, embodies the spiritual gift of exhortation like no other person I have known. This book chronicles the testimony of a woman whose faith has been tested greatly yet developed deeply. She writes as I have watched her live—with a contagious courage and confidence in an omnicompetent God. Her passion is to inspire others to that same faith and hope. Rooted in the definition of the word *restore* are the ideas of return, repair, and renew. All of these speak of the work God desires to perform in our lives, and these are the ever-available gifts of God this book is all about.

—*Dr. Mark L. Bailey,* chancellor and senior professor
of Bible exposition, Dallas Theological Seminary

I have known Cindy as a close friend since we met in high school forty-five-plus years ago. Cindy has always had a competitive and compassionate spirit instilled in her by both parents. The obstacles she has overcome to restore her own life have only strengthened her faith and willingness to help others. The restorative power of moving forward with faith and trust in God is a message we all need to share during these pivotal and tumultuous times.

—*Robert H. Dedman Jr.,* GP of Putterboy (Pinehurst) Ltd.

For anyone who is in a season of life when they are thirsty for some encouragement, inspiration, motivation, and hope, open any chapter in Cindy Brinker Simmons's book, *Restored: Reconnecting Life's Broken Pieces,* and be quenched. She uses wit and humor and wisdom straight from the Bible as well as her personal experience. Not filled with cliches but packed with practical help to answer life's hard questions. I strongly recommend you read it.

—*Susan Perlman,* chief partnership officer, Jews for Jesus

Restored is going to change hearts. It speaks to me on so many levels. Its pages brought chills down my back, tears to my eyes, and a smile to my soul! In such a masterful way, Cindy's compassionate and powerful words provide hope, joy, and faith to a broken world. I love this book!

—*Billy Dawson,* Nashville country artist, songwriter, and producer

In the years since our UVA tennis connection brought us together, Cindy has been a tremendous mentor, friend, and uniquely positive force in my life. Her resilience, kindness, openness, and deep faith in the Lord inspire me and shine brightly through the message she shares in this book. With her faith at the forefront and through a touching, in-depth account of her own experience, Cindy models how we can triumph over loss and hardship with which each of us will inevitably contend. I am awed by Cindy's resilience and delighted to know that many more people will have the opportunity to be inspired by her story.

—*Sara O'Leary,* University of Virginia women's tennis head coach

In your hands is Cindy Brinker Simmons's gift to the broken heart. It is well entitled, *Restored: Reconnecting Life's Broken Pieces.* Indeed, the storms of life can shake souls and raise hard questions about God and the meaning of life itself. Yet in the midst of turmoil, there's wisdom, strength, and encouragement for those who know where to seek it. Cindy shows us that these can be found in Scripture. Moreover, her practical guidance and transparent accounts of tennis, trials, tragedies, and triumphs will bless your heart and encourage your walk of faith. If a tornado has just torn through your life, *Restored* offers the spiritual help and joyful hope you've been longing for.

—*Dr. Peter A. Lillback,* founder and president emeritus,
Providence Forum; president,
Westminster Theological Seminary, Philadelphia

Cindy provides hope for those in the most challenging of times. Her own experiences, determination, faith, and trust are an inspiration for anyone seeking restoration. Carefully researched and drawing on figures from C. S. Lewis to Moses and Bob Dylan, Cindy's journey is a roadmap for purpose and peace.

—*Jane McGarry,* Good Morning Texas host;
National Gracie Award "Best Local Anchor"

Restored: Reconnecting Life's Broken Pieces is a beautifully presented work that draws from the author's personal experiences with loss and devastation as opposed to a theoretical essay on how to process through seemingly hopeless situations. She uses her inner coach to explain how to reset lost momentum and stay in the game. Anyone in the midst of physical, relational, or spiritual despair will be encouraged to gain hope and joy out of the depths of brokenness.

> —**Del Harris,** NBA coach; Naismith Basketball Hall of Fame

I have never met anyone more enthusiastic and encouraging about life than Cindy and am excited to see her impact on others through *Restored.* While it's difficult to see at times, God always has a plan, and Cindy shares a path to hope and joy in *Restored.* This is a must read for all who thirst for a fulfilling life.

> —**Dirk P. Katstra,** University of Virginia, senior executive director, principal gifts; former executive director, Virginia Athletics Foundation

Cindy speaks truth in her insights that really blessed me, but her deep desire is simply to honor Jesus Christ in all she writes and shares with us. Cindy ties God's ways together for us and encourages us that the goals of His heart ... are our greatest purpose this side of heaven. Please read Cindy's message.

> —**John M. Maisel,** founder and chairman emeritus, East-West Ministries

RESTORED

RECONNECTING LIFE'S BROKEN PIECES

RESTORED

RECONNECTING LIFE'S BROKEN PIECES

CINDY BRINKER SIMMONS

REDEMPTION PRESS

Published by Redemption Press, PO Box 427, Enumclaw, WA 98022.

(360) 226-3488

Redemption Press is honored to present this title in partnership with the author. The views expressed or implied in this work are those of the author. Redemption Press provides our imprint seal representing design excellence, creative content, and high-quality production.

ISBN 13: 978-1-951350-57-4 (Paperback)
978-1-951350-58-1 (Hard cover)
978-1-951350-59-8 (ePUB)

Library of Congress Catalog Card Number: 2023917151

ALSO BY THE AUTHOR

Little Mo's Legacy: A Mother's Lessons, A Daughter's Story

Net proceeds from *Restored* will be donated to Wipe Out Kids' Cancer (www.wokc.org) and the Maureen Connolly Brinker Tennis Foundation (www.mcbtennis.org).

God is in His heaven;

He does as He pleases,

and He does right well.

Favorite words of praise and adoration to God

from my beloved Bob inspired by

Psalm 115:3

To my beloved husband, Bob,
who faithfully modeled the perseverance, joy, and hope
that are shared among these pages.
Bob lived and loved well as he showed a watching world that his trust,
no matter the circumstances, was always firmly anchored
in his Lord and Savior, Jesus Christ.
He is dearly missed!

To our treasured son, William,
who loved his courageous and humble daddy
and now has grown to be a wise, talented, and strong young man
with a robust faith fully focused on Jesus.

I give praise with a heart full of gratitude and awe
for the holy and righteous King of kings
who has blessed me beyond measure with my cherished Bob and William
and with the indescribable gift of His Son, Jesus Christ.

CONTENTS

INTRODUCTION

In the early 1950s, a teenager from California awed the world with her dazzling and powerful tennis finesse. At the age of sixteen, Maureen "Little Mo" Connolly became the youngest female player to win the US Open. She won three straight Wimbledon titles in 1952, 1953, and 1954 and was the reigning world champion in women's tennis during those years. She was the first woman, and still the only American woman, to achieve the prestigious calendar Grand Slam title (winning all four major tennis championships in one calendar year). Only five players in the history of tennis have accomplished that coveted victory. A horseback riding accident abruptly ended her meteoric career in 1954—all before she was twenty years of age. In 1955, Maureen married, then had two daughters within the next four years and was impacting lives from her myriad personal and professional pursuits. In 1969, at the age of thirty-four, she died from ovarian cancer. While her adoring public called her Little Mo, I simply called her Mom. I was twelve when she died.

I married my best friend and the love of my life, Bob Simmons, in 1990. We had a treasured son five and a half years later and were preparing to adopt a little girl from Russia to expand our family. However, our plans were indefinitely put on hold when Bob was diagnosed with a rare cancer in 2002. He passed away in 2005.

Life is hard. No one is immune from the bumps and bruises of daily living. It is called suffering, and it can be very painful. We have all been there. It has been said that you are either in a crisis, leaving a crisis, or about to enter a crisis. Suffering is part of life's universal experience.

Sometimes it is really hard to take that first step when life weighs too much. Psychologically, you are frazzled. Emotionally, you are drained. Physically, you are exhausted. As each uninvited hardship busts through your life, you cry out, "God, what is going on? Have You forgotten me? Is this Your plan for my life? *Really?*"

Your emotions and faith are shredded as you call out to God in a bewildered state of disbelief, outrage, and discouragement. But on you must go. Your feet want to move forward, but they are stuck on life's hold button.

Restored: Reconnecting Life's Broken Pieces is about two worlds colliding. One, the great excitement of expectation. The other, a harsh wreckage of reality. It is where faith and disbelief intersect. For so many, life operates at this crossroads. Hope is detoured and derailed at this fragile fork in the road. Discouragement and helplessness keep us safely atop the heap of rubbish that used to be our fondest aspirations, ambitions, and anticipations. Our brokenness is unable to comprehend any plan or purpose for our life. Even our faith, if we have one, is buried in the wasteland of hopelessness.

This book authentically wrestles with the reality of that dark place where doubt, fear, and sadness reside but encourages readers that hope is found there too. *Restored* will reinvigorate the spirit of those who need to be refreshed and strengthened. It will motivate those who need life breathed back into them. In short, it will remind each reader to move forward because every life has a plan and a purpose. Missteps can find themselves redirected onto paths leading to great benefits never expected.

Few long journeys go exactly according to plan. They have detours and delays, typically cost more than expected, and take more energy than was imagined. However, trials can be treasures in disguise. Some of life's greatest blessings are hidden under layers of suffering, but you must persevere to find them. The journey is tough, but the testing is designed for your own endurance, maturity, and good.

My prayer as you read *Restored* is that you make an important discovery: God is always present. He walks with you, carries you, and never leaves you. Restoration happens by trusting in God's ways, in His timing, and in His unwavering love. His purposes and plans for you are good—even when your circumstances are not.

Restored emphasizes the importance of productive, meaningful relationships to help you walk robustly through a world that is falling apart. God knows. To a broken people living centuries ago who were caught up in this same kind of chaos, confusion, and calamity, He whispered a promise. He whispers the same to you right now.

> I know what I'm doing. I have it all planned out—plans
> to take care of you, not abandon you, plans to give
> you the future you hope for. (Jeremiah 29:11 MSG)

In the pages that follow, let's discover together what that promise means for you today.

SECTION 1

CINDY'S STORY

"This Can't Be Happening!"

So you're in a bad place.

Some unexpected twister tore a path across your life, leaving ugly debris and mangled pieces in its wake. Lying among the wreckage is your fabulous future, buried under the shattered hopes and dreams your heart yearned for … once upon a time.

What happened? Perhaps you've been wounded by your own mistakes or choices. Perhaps by some bewildering, even devastating, circumstance. Perhaps your brokenness wasn't your fault at all; perhaps someone whom you trusted betrayed, rejected, or mistreated you. Perhaps this tornado is no one's fault but is simply a tragic turn of events you read about happening to others—only this time it knocked *your* front door in and wreaked havoc inside.

But no matter what has brought on this adversity, you feel alone and disconnected from yourself, from others, and from God. Candidly, you may feel like God is angry at you, that He blames you for this mess and holds you responsible.

I get it. At twelve years old, my life unraveled just like this. For many years, I tried every way I knew possible to restore the broken pieces.

An Unexpected Storm

It wasn't always that way for me. In fact, you might say that my little sister, Brenda, and I had a pretty sweet life in the years before the twister hit. We knew our parents loved us.

There were the trips to Disneyland, the World's Fair, and the San Diego Zoo. We enjoyed swimming parties, birthday parties, and holiday parties— really, any reason to have a fun party! Family dinners were special with laughter, engaging conversations, and dessert following every meal. We had a two-tone station wagon, so popular in the 1960s, parked in front of our two-story home in the suburbs of Dallas, Texas. Tallyrand, our chocolate poodle, and Max, our floppy-eared German shepherd, completed our active family.

Life is good. Except when it isn't.

Then came my mom's cancer diagnosis. Since cancer wasn't talked about in those days, Brenda and I never knew she was sick.

Mom thought she could beat it, but she didn't. In three years, my vibrant hero succumbed to ovarian cancer. She was thirty-four. I was twelve. Brenda was ten. Life came to an abrupt halt.

At Mom's funeral, I visualized our family as a one-thousand-piece jigsaw puzzle thrown haphazardly to the wind. I thought, *How are we even going to find these pieces, much less put them back together again?* In the aftermath of the storm, our home felt like a giant vacuum cleaner had descended from the heavenlies and sucked all the joy from within its walls. Even Tallyrand, who routinely greeted Mom in the driveway when she drove her gold-and-white Riviera into the garage, stopped waiting for her when she no longer emerged from the car. Our sweet poodle died within the year—I'm convinced of a broken heart.

Life just stopped. I was terrified. I knew the ache I felt in my heart was there to stay.

What Had I Done to Deserve This?

Without a doubt, I believed God hated me. Candidly, I have no idea why I would have embraced that thought. Dad was supportive, encouraging, and nurturing as we settled into a new normal life without Mom. But I reasoned I must have done something so bad, so wrong, so terrible that God was punishing me by taking my mom. After all, I was the only kid I knew who didn't have a mom. I really thought God hated me. Quite honestly, I wasn't too crazy about Him either!

Have you ever felt like that? Have you ever thought your bad decisions or irresponsible actions generated the permanent wrath of a vengeful God? That there was no way out of His lingering punishment?

Even if you couldn't quite put your finger on it or even if it wasn't your fault, somehow or in some way, you must have done *something* bad enough to activate God's fury.

Or maybe you have felt God was inactive. Inconsistent. Indifferent. That He never heard your prayers, much less answered them.

Worse yet, have you ever thought you were so far from Him you could never regain His love? Be forgiven? Be accepted?

That was the dwelling place for my twelve-year-old head and my heart—on the heap of a wasteland where circumstances and grief collided and hopelessness crashed. I had a sense I could do nothing that would be good enough to win back the affections of this angry God whom I had somehow managed to infuriate.

The guilt that I had caused my mother's death weighed heavily on me. At this sweet, young age, I suddenly had a gaping hole in my heart no EKG would ever detect. The loss anchored the guilt there.

My Plan to Win Back God's Love

How could I earn back the love of an outraged God? I reasoned I must perform for His affection. And not just perform, but perform *well*. I needed to win! After all, I knew God couldn't love a loser. So I pursued performance with a vengeance, perhaps the same vengeance with which I thought God had pursued me.

Winning was part of my family's history. While in her later years Mom was just Little Mom to Brenda and me, to her adoring public, Maureen Connolly was affectionately known as Little Mo, nicknamed by famed sports journalist Nelson Fisher after the powerful battleship USS *Missouri*, also known as the Big Mo. Mr. Fisher compared Little Mo's groundstrokes, which he said rendered her opponents shell shocked, to the explosive firepower of *Missouri*. Little Mo was the number one female tennis player in the world in 1952, 1953, and 1954. She was named Female Athlete of the Year by the Associated Press for three consecutive years (1951–53).

However, Little Mo's competitive career ended abruptly with a horseback riding accident in July 1954 as she prepared to defend her fourth US Open title. But after the accident, she married, became a mother, and continued to impact the tennis world as a commentator, coach, and cofounder of the Maureen Connolly Brinker Tennis Foundation—all with an astounding spirit of giftedness, grace, and giving back to her beloved sport.

Mom never wanted me to play tennis. She wanted to shield me from the immense pressure of following in a famous parent's footsteps. Yet I was relentless in wanting to take up the sport. I was destined to play tennis. It was in my blood. So she agreed to let me play when I was eleven.

After her death, tennis was one way I felt connected to Mom. I practiced with a passionate fervor driven by grief and the need to keep her memory alive. Three hours after school. All weekends. Soon I was competing in a constant stream of tournaments. Within two years, I battled in national tournaments from the East Coast to the West Coast. At age fourteen, I ranked as the top junior in my age division in Texas and in the top ten to fifteen in the country. I never looked back.

How I wanted those wins! Dad built trophy shelves on one entire wall in my bedroom to display all the awards won in those years following Mom's death. With each victory, I was sure I could earn not only a trophy but a thumbs-up from God.

Riding the Performance Merry-Go-Round

My drive to win God back spilled over into other areas of my young life. In the middle of my ninth-grade year, I was enrolled in an excellent private school known for its very rigorous academic curriculum. Both my accelerated tennis career and challenging course load fostered my extreme sense of performance. Propelled by my desire to please God on this fast track, I dove in!

As with any performance-driven outcome, when I succeeded, things felt really good. I was popular, respected, and having fun. But that contentment could be fleeting. Grades, tennis competitions, and the relationship dramas of a high-school-age girl put me on an emotional merry-go-round, and I was getting motion sickness for all my efforts to be acceptable in God's sight. Sometimes I felt discouraged knowing I could never perform well enough. It reminded me of my pet hamster running like crazy on that big wheel that just went round and round in his cage. It gave him the feeling of forward movement, but he never went anywhere! That poor little fellow must have been pooped! At times, I experienced the same exhaustion and frustration of chasing after God's approval.

The Test That Changed Everything

On top of everything, I really missed Mom. I couldn't figure out this whole death thing. I had heard of heaven but wasn't sure what it looked like or how you got there. Confused, I wanted answers.

But I was moving forward, encouraged by my accomplishments, and sometimes forgetting about God entirely. I kept winning tournaments and doing well in school … until a class in tenth grade literally brought me to my knees. I secretly hoped a three-week, pass/fail, elective religion class would generate some solutions to the pain nagging at my heart.

However, no enlightenment happened during those three weeks except for one major shakeup—the day before the pass/fail test, I realized I was clueless about the material! I was convinced I would fail the test, and that would implode my good GPA. In desperation, I drove to my dad's office because he had a beautiful way of calming me down in stressful moments like these.

When I told Dad about my religion test the next day, he said a woman who worked for him could perhaps help me. Her father was a pastor. I told him she couldn't *possibly* help me because she hadn't taken the class! Dad didn't buy it. I soon sat face-to-face with a preacher's daughter!

She asked me about my personal and spiritual life. I filled an hour on the former topic and about twenty-two seconds on the latter one. She told me that God loved me so much … that I didn't have to perform for Him … that He loved me no matter how well (or poorly) I did.

Really? My identity and self-worth were so wrapped up in tennis and grades that I was shocked at that concept. Furthermore, she told me I could do nothing to earn my way into heaven. A holy God could only allow perfection into heaven, and based on my own merits, I knew I didn't make that cut! She said that we all sin and fall short of the glory of God, so *no one* could get into heaven based on his or her own virtues. God's solution was radical—He loved us so unconditionally that He sent His Son, Jesus Christ, to die for our sins. She said it was an agonizing death on a cross—Jesus was crucified.

God *loved* me? He sent His Son to *die* for me? I couldn't imagine God making such a sacrifice for me.

And, she said, God's love for me was the same at my birth as it was when Mom took her last breath on this side of heaven. There was no condemnation. No punishment. No direct hit.

In that moment, I made the most crucial decision of my life. I got down on my knees and accepted Jesus Christ as my Lord and Savior. Putting my faith and trust in Jesus assured my eternal destination in heaven.

I felt immediately set free! An enormous weight lifted from my heart and shoulders. I did not have to win tennis matches, make As on my tests, or be the best at what I was doing to win God's favor. He loves me … all the time … despite myself and despite my circumstances.

And, as importantly, He will never leave or forsake me. That night, I savored the outrageous grace of God and the peace of being loved so completely by Him. (And, yes, the next day I passed my test!)

God's Exclamation Point

Life took on a new splendor. I graduated from high school and attended the University of Virginia, competing on both the women's tennis and cross-country teams. I received some honors and accolades at Virginia but, more importantly, completed my academics with calm contentment. It was a glorious four years!

I returned to Dallas and worked at a country club as its public relations, special events, and membership director. I attended a few Bible studies that deepened my faith and my love for God. A few ministries even asked me to join their boards. Dallas was a good place for me to land.

One evening at Bible study, a charming young man walked in and captured my attention.

His presence and good looks totally mesmerized me, in addition to his kind and gentle demeanor. His name was Bob Simmons, and over the next seven years, our friendship grew. God used those years to show me the compassion of his heart, the depth of his wisdom, and the authenticity of his faith. Bob didn't care about performance and focused on meeting the needs of people where they were, with no fanfare or concern about recognition. He just lived to love others. I was awed by his genuine humility and personal integrity.

After those seven years, a fire was ignited in our hearts, and we married in 1990. Bob was my best friend and the love of my life. He called me "sweetie pie," and I called him "beloved." We had William, our treasured son, five and a half years later and were preparing to adopt a little girl from Russia to expand our family in 2002.

Life was good. We were on lots of invitation lists, had treasured friendships, and were very active with our church, charity, and ministry work. Our professional lives were also very fulfilling and robust. We truly felt God's favor.

A Change in Plans

And then, when plans were being made for our little girl's adoption, William's graduation from kindergarten, and some thrilling new business partnerships for Bob, that brutal twister blew back into our lives with one statement: "Bob, you have cancer."

Cancer again invaded the inner sanctum of my home thirty-three years later. How could this be happening? It took three painstakingly long weeks to diagnose Bob's rare cancer. His prognosis was grim—three months to live. As we left the oncologist's office with that devastating news, Bob said,

"Sweetie pie, I don't know if I have three months, three years, or thirty years. But whatever time I do have, from this moment forward, we will glorify God!"

In his heartbreak, Bob gave us a mission statement: we will honor God by choosing joy because we fully trust Him. And that is what we did. We shared our faith in the Lord boldly and bravely. We declared this adversity was part of God's sovereign purpose. Our peace and joy grew as our trust exponentially expanded. And people responded. Lives were changed. Hearts were drawn to Jesus Christ. Our victory over our misery infused hope into a watching world. The three-month death sentence turned into three years on our cancer journey. Bob died in 2005.

A Matter of Perspective

Besides tending to my aching heart, I had to nurture, comfort, and encourage William, who was nine when his daddy was called Home. When Bob was given a terminal prognosis, we determined not to be influenced by man's prediction but to be obedient to God's calling. We would not allow cancer to define us because we trusted God's plan for our lives and for William's. This time, as the twister blew through our home and my heart, I knew Bob's sad loss was part of God's eternal design rather than His ferocious fury being hurled at me.

What About You?

It's true what they say: most people are either going through a crisis, coming out of a crisis, or heading into one. As long as we have breath, some past, present, or future sorrow can cause us to hyperventilate. But it doesn't have to be that way. We all have our own story, plan, and purpose that God has set in motion. Perhaps today you are facing some seismic struggle. If not, you are blessed. At some point in the future (or perhaps already in the past), some unwelcome crisis will come crashing into your life. Whether you had anything to do with it or not, the way you respond to that circumstance can leave you victorious or defeated.

At age twelve, when I lost my mom, the struggle in my relationship with God kept me from moving forward in a meaningful and healthy way. More than three decades later, in the middle of another great loss, my love for God and my trust in Him allowed me to choose joy even when my circumstances screamed of heartbreak and grief. My faith was not shaken and my hope not dismantled even though my loss was excruciating.

When painful events happen, you can ask tough questions. How you answer those questions can significantly impact the way you look at yourself, others, and God. You might be asking these very questions now:

- How do I regain wholeness after this devastating heartbreak?
- How can I reconcile relationships lost in the crisis—or even before?
- How do I resolve these feelings of hopelessness and sadness?
- How can I repair what has been broken?
- How can I reconnect with myself, others, and God?
- How can I restore a sense of belonging to someone, to something, or to somewhere?

These tough questions demand responses. Let's lean in together and discover the answers. My hope and prayer are that they change your life … as they have mine.

SECTION 2

CHAPTER 1

RESTORING MOMENTUM

Stuck on Hold

My dear friend Betty Lovell and I were talking one evening. We have known each other for over thirty years. Three decades covers a lot of miles! Loads of laughter and good times. But this time wasn't one of those "singing from the mountaintop" moments. Betty had just completed a tough surgery and was dealing with an aging parent with dementia. The weightiness of both situations was uncomfortably pressing down. Betty said, "There have been many times when I felt my life was on the hold button, and that button just got stuck!"

Betty was a modern-day prophet without even knowing it. Yes! Life does have a hold button. We all experience it. That season can be a day or two, or it can be prolonged for months or even years. Recovery can be a slow, painful process.

Has that happened to you … lately? Has your world been rocked? Right now, does it seem the only thing you can do is to take deep breaths and try to grasp what has just happened? That is OK. Pausing can be good. Life's hold button has its purpose. Sometimes we just need to rest and recover. Taking time to recuperate is important to healing. But there comes a time when you must move forward. There is a moment when you are propelled to get back in the game even when your body or your mind or your emotions are still reeling from being a direct hit on the bull's-eye. You can't stay in neutral forever. You don't want to remain stuck on hold indefinitely. Life is beckoning …

What Does God Say to Do?

God is a God of action. He called creation into being. He breathed His breath of life into man. He rules with authority. He never slumbers. He is on the move! He calls you to do the same. And He calls you to move on from the past. Push away the regrets and past circumstances. Do not dwell on events from long ago that paralyze you. He wants you to start moving!

Scripture speaks:

> Forget the former things; do not dwell on the past.
> (Isaiah 43:18)

> Forgetting what is behind and straining toward what is ahead, I press on toward the goal to win the prize for which God has called me heavenward in Christ Jesus. (Philippians 3:13–14)

God's goal is always your restoration and redemption. He wants you to show up, keep moving, and press forward. The important thing to remember is that God is with you. Future king David wrote in Psalm 23:4, "Even though I walk through the valley of the shadow of death, I will fear no evil, for you are with me; your rod and your staff, they comfort me."

How can you restore momentum to your days? Remember that the grace, love, and support of God are always present. So keep moving in pursuit of God's call. He beckons you and will direct your steps.

Just a Reminder

But before you get started on your journey, life offers you three different directional options. Your first option is to move backward. When you do nothing, isolate yourself, or refuse to move forward, the backward slide can gain momentum over time and bury you in hopelessness and despair.

Your second option is to stay in place. Like on a treadmill, you may feel a sense of movement, but you aren't going anywhere! You become exhausted and discouraged because your momentum is creating no forward progress. You are *doing* but feel no personal fulfillment, satisfaction, or achievement because you are stuck in the same place.

Your final option is to move forward. Nothing is achieved by looking in the rearview mirror forever. To pursue your dreams, for relationships to deepen, and for emotions to be healthy, you must gain momentum. To experience victory, you must move forward. When you do, you'll see results occur, milestones reached, and goals met—but only when you advance rather than get stuck in neutral or slide backward. When you begin to move, even slowly, you restore momentum. Remember to just start simply … and then to simply start. Life is a marathon and not a sprint. Most importantly, God calls you to run the race!

Facing Fear

How can you restore that forward movement? Start by facing your fear. As you launch your journey, you can encounter a debilitating roadblock. Its name is fear. It is a malicious tool that the enemy uses with great effectiveness. Truly, fear can be one of the biggest barricades to moving forward.

The words *fear*, *afraid*, and *terrified* are mentioned more than five hundred times in the Old and New Testaments. God must consider this a top priority to address!

My mother told me that when she walked onto the tennis court, she was faced with two options—wanting to win or fearing to lose. Both approaches were aimed at victory, but the mindset was different. If she was fixated on the fear of losing, she would be doomed before she hit the first ball. She would be paralyzed from making the big shots and would play tentatively. Her mental quickness would be compromised. That was not an option for Little Mo! She wanted to win! She was self-assured, bold, and alert. There was no inhibition in her play. She could hit winners under pressure. Fear holds you back. Confidence is liberating and compels you forward with great passion and courage.

Trust God ... One Step at a Time

So how do you overcome fear? How do you replace panic with peace? Concern with calm? When your heart is racing, your throat is parched, and you are feeling light-headed? Bible teacher Beth Moore says to "do it scared"[1] to encourage her audiences to just put one foot in front of the other even if they are fearful. She said that we must press through our fear to secure what God has for us to possess.

Trapped at the Red Sea with mountains to the right and left and Pharaoh's army closing in behind them, the Israelites were rocked with fear. There was no exit strategy in this geographic cul-de-sac. I can only imagine the wails for help and cries of despair on the bank of the Red Sea from the two million Israelites whom Moses had just led out of bondage in Egypt! Moses had told the distraught Israelites in Exodus 14:13, "Do not be afraid. Stand firm and you will see the deliverance the LORD will bring you today." Moses knew the Lord could be trusted to deliver the Israelites from this seemingly impossible situation. But their fear and trembling were paralyzing any belief in God's rescue plan, and they had even less hope of surviving their impending dire circumstance.

At this point in Exodus 14:15, we read, "Then the LORD said to Moses, 'Why are you crying out to me? Tell the Israelites to move on.'" While the Israelites could only see the vastness of the Red Sea through to the horizon, God had promised to give them land on the opposite shore. God's miraculous rescue plan was to part the Red Sea and let them walk to the other side. Can you imagine the faces of the Israelites as they watched the Red Sea divide and form translucent walls of water on the right and left sides to create an avenue of escape from the advancing Egyptians? Even the most skeptical Israelites in that wilderness throng were silenced in amazed awe and in worshipful praise as they saw God's exit strategy play out. Then, step by step, they trusted God and walked into the midst of the sea throughout the night and early morning until they were all safely on the opposite shore of the Red Sea.

Trust is a powerful word. It demands full surrender to someone or something that will, ultimately, create a hopeful outcome for you. The Bible says you should place your trust *only* in God, your audience of One.

> Trust in the LORD with all your heart and lean not
> on your own understanding; in all your ways
> acknowledge him, and he will make your paths
> straight. (Proverbs 3:5–6)

> Trust in the LORD forever, for the LORD, the LORD, is the
> Rock eternal. (Isaiah 26:4)

> Some trust in chariots and some in horses, but we
> trust in the name of the LORD our God. (Psalm 20:7)

God is without equal. He is perfect. He is all-knowing. He is holy. But most importantly, He loves you. He cares for you. Since the beginning of His creation, He is your refuge. In His own words, He declares, "I have loved you with an everlasting love; I have drawn you with loving-kindness" (Jeremiah 31:3).

God is the only One worthy of our worship. He is the only One to rely or depend upon. He is the only One with the strength, ability, and wisdom with whom to place your confidence every minute of every day. Leaning into His presence provides peace, assurance, and hope and gives you the courage to trust Him for the next step.

Keep Moving!

God says, "Go get it! It's right there!" You must have the strength to get what God wants to give you and to keep it. He has your best interests at heart and desires for you to live your days with hope and great expectation. But you need to be on guard to prevent the enemy from coming back for it.

Chinese philosopher Lao Tzu (c. 604 BC–c. 531 BC) famously wrote, "A journey of a thousand miles begins with a single step."[2] All treks begin with a starting point and then that first step. However, you need to keep moving forward to make any possible progress.

Despite trembling knees and sweaty palms, God's grace is ample to get you through. Even if you are scared, if you are doing the will of God, He will not forsake you in that faithful act of obedience. When it seems the gates of hell are breaking wide open, keep moving forward! The slightest momentum forward can jump-start your courage and inspire your resolve to take the next step … and the next … and the next.

And since God never leaves you, the outcome is providentially in His hands. Even if the result is not what you wanted, there is a bigger purpose in it—a purpose that you might not be able to see or understand until you reach the other side of heaven. But you can be assured that His plan for you is good—even when it hurts. Nothing is wasted in fulfilling God's purpose.

Be Confident in God's Provision!

Go to battle emboldened with the courage of a warrior under God's watchful command, not a fearful soldier working alone. And when those moments of fear and trembling come, you know that God empowers you. Young David boldly faced Goliath, the nine-foot Philistine warrior. Rather than his knees knocking, David was confident that he had the power of the Lord with him and that God would deliver Goliath over to him. Even though the battle confrontation between the giant champion and the boy looked hopelessly mismatched, David never wavered and anticipated victory.

As he faced Goliath, David said, "You come against me with sword and spear and javelin, but I come against you in the name of the LORD Almighty, the God of the armies of Israel, whom you have defied. This day the LORD will hand you over to me, and I'll strike you down and cut off your head" (1 Samuel 17:45–46).

There was nothing cowardly or spineless in that statement! David's confidence was focused on his assurance that the power of the Lord would deliver him the victory rather than placing trust in his own talents to prevail.

You can't do it alone. There will be times—many times—when the stress, wear, and tear of life are imposing and seemingly insurmountable. But you are equipped to face those times with a greater sense of courage and resolve knowing God is with you. Trust Him, no matter the circumstance. He is the One who will direct your steps—one step at a time—even when you are outwitted, outnumbered, and outflanked. By trusting in God's power and might to carry you, boldly walk onto the battlefield—wanting to win!

Call Satan Out

Let's not ignore the elephant in the room. Satan is your enemy, and he seeks to annihilate you.

John 10:10 reveals his evil job description: "The thief comes only to steal and kill and destroy."

That's right. The enemy wants to defeat you, flatten you, consume you. He is not on your team. He wants to take from you what God has so graciously given you. He wants you to stay stuck in your defeat. Paralyzed by your fear. Robbed of your joy. He wants to claim your life for eternal doom and darkness.

The Bible warns us, "Do not give the devil a foothold" (Ephesians 4:27). In other words, if the enemy has the slightest grip on your life, he will effectively use sin to wreak havoc on you personally and, in turn, will bring about even greater destruction in the lives of others.

That's the bad news.

The good news is that Satan has no authority over God. Satan knows that. The Bible says, "You believe that there is one God. Good! Even the demons believe that—and shudder" (James 2:19). The enemy has no power over God. Satan trembles, shakes, and convulses at the very thought of God. The enemy knows his evil schemes cannot be effective against such sovereignty and supremacy. If you are walking with God, Satan has no power over you.

The second part of John 10:10 reveals the beautiful job description of Jesus: "I have come that they may have life, and have it to the full." The evil one desires chaos, calamity, and destruction. The Lord wants restoration, peace, and fulfillment for you.

So acknowledge Satan for who he is—a thug, thief, and murderer. The Bible calls him "a liar and the father of lies" (John 8:44). Call him out! Do not let him have any authority over you! When you feel oppressed, demeaned, or hopeless and are unable to move forward, speak the name of Jesus over yourself. Call on His presence to protect you. The Word of God is your refuge, shield, and fortress. You walk in victory, and every step forward tramples the enemy's plan to undo you. Let Satan know he is in your rearview mirror. Gone. Evicted. Exiled from your life. He has no power over you. Put him on notice … now!

Staying in the Game

What is next to keep that momentum going? Staying in the game!

February 1, 2015. The outcome of Super Bowl XLIX was on the line between the Seattle Seahawks and the New England Patriots. The Seahawks had the ball on the Patriots' one-yard line with twenty-six seconds remaining in the game. The score was 28–24 in favor of the Patriots. Just one more yard, and the Seahawks would score! Seahawks quarterback Russell Wilson threw a pass intended for Ricardo Lockette. Out of nowhere, Patriot defensive player Malcolm Butler intercepted the pass at the goal line! The Patriots maintained their 28–24 lead in the waning seconds and won the game! But the real story is what happened two plays earlier. With a minute left in the game, Wilson threw a pass to Jermaine Kearse. Malcolm Butler was covering Kearse and reached to intercept the ball but tipped it instead. The deflected ball was caught by Kearse on the Patriots' five-yard line. After that stunning catch, the Seahawks were five yards away from scoring. Butler did not let that botched interception discourage him. He didn't falter. He kept his head in the game. Two plays later, he intercepted Wilson's pass from the one-yard line in what is considered one of the greatest clutch plays in Super Bowl history. What seemed an inevitable loss two plays earlier turned into an unimaginable victory for the Patriots.

Question: What would have happened if Malcolm Butler had been distraught after his deflected ball caused Jermaine Kearse's remarkable catch with the game on the line? What if Butler had been so shattered that he could not have gotten mentally back in the game? What if he had accused himself of being shamefully incompetent and had prematurely blamed himself for the Patriots' loss, paralyzing his play for the rest of the game? If those toxic thoughts had prevented Butler from mentally staying in the game, most assuredly the Super Bowl's Vince Lombardi Trophy would have had a different 2015 champion engraved on it.

Rosa Parks (1913–2005) has been called "the first lady of civil rights" and "the mother of the freedom movement" for her pivotal role in the Montgomery bus boycott in 1955.

Montgomery, Alabama, had passed a city ordinance in 1900 that segregated bus passengers by race. While white passengers could sit in the front of the bus, the "colored" section was for the Black passengers in the back of the bus. The ordinance required Black people to give up their seats to a white person if the bus was full and a white passenger entered the bus.

On December 1, 1955, Rosa Parks refused to give up her seat and stand when requested to do so by the bus driver once the bus filled and white people entered the bus. Her refusal led to her arrest. She was charged and found guilty of violating the segregation law of the Montgomery city code and of disorderly conduct.

Mrs. Parks was a well-respected, hardworking, and dignified Black woman in the Montgomery community. She appealed her conviction and formally challenged the legality of racial segregation. Her arrest activated Black leaders in Montgomery to prompt the Black community to boycott public bus usage on the day of her trial, December 5, 1955. The Montgomery bus boycott was so successful that day that the Montgomery Improvement Association (MIA) was immediately established to manage the city's boycott and to take advantage of the momentum achieved, electing twenty-six-year-old Martin Luther King Jr. as its first president. The boycott lasted for over a year and crippled Montgomery's bus transit system since more than 75% of their ridership was from the Black community. Ultimately, the Supreme Court ruled in November 1956 that bus segregation was unconstitutional.

Question: What would have happened if Rosa Parks had complied with the demand of the bus driver to get up and move from her seat, as did the other three Black passengers sitting next to her? What if she had been consumed by the immediate thought of the hostility, challenges, and scorn she would receive if she didn't move? What if she thought this needed to be someone else's crusade for another day because she was comfortable enough in her life and didn't want the hardships that would result from her actions? Mrs. Parks suffered death threats and was fired from her seamstress job after her arrest, but she continued her valiant crusade to be a catalyst in the civil rights movement and a national icon of resistance to racial segregation.

In her own words in a National Public Radio interview in 1992, Mrs. Parks said, "I had not planned to get arrested. I had plenty to do without having to end up in jail. But when I had to face that decision, I didn't hesitate to do so because I felt we had endured that too long. The more we gave in, the more we complied with that kind of treatment, the more oppressive it became."[3] It is amazing how great movements in history have relied on people staying the course even when distress, difficulty, and danger have key roles in the drama.

Oskar Schindler (1908–74) was a German industrialist and member of the Nazi Party during World War II. He owned enamelware and ammunition factories during the war, employing Jews because they were cheaper to pay than other workers. Originally, Schindler was an opportunist and sought to prosper through his factories. His attitude changed as he witnessed the cruelty of the Nazis exterminating the Jews. When his Jewish factory workers were threatened with deportation to death camps, Schindler gave black market gifts or bribes to Nazi officials to rescue his employees. He is credited with saving twelve hundred Jews during the Holocaust by writing their names on a list of *essential* employees. Schindler saved thousands more Jews from death camps throughout the war. He lost his entire fortune to save his workers during the war.

Question: What would have happened to the thousands of Jews caught in the terror of Hitler's Third Reich if Oskar Schindler had been paralyzed by fear that his actions were too dangerous? What would have happened if he had prioritized his personal wealth and comfort over the lives of the Jews he saved? What would have happened if the massiveness of his rescue plan had overwhelmed him and he had not courageously and boldly extended his hand to sacrificially save his doomed workers? For Schindler, staying in the game was mandatory even when it was highly probable that he would personally suffer from his selfless efforts to save others. Historical accounting of World War II would have been different if Schindler had not stepped up. Millions of Jews, more than three and a half generations later, would not be alive today if Schindler had not stuck steadfastly to his plan to save their ancestors. The impact of courage is sobering.

History has chronicled what happens when heroes step forward. Ordinary people doing extraordinary things in extreme circumstances when the stakes are high. Rosa Parks, Oskar Schindler, and Malcolm Butler are no different from you and me. They were faced with circumstances that demanded action—either charging forward or retreating in fear, doubt, or discouragement. You face challenges every day. They might not play out in the Super Bowl or change the course of history, but they can define your life.

Victory involves staying in the game, my friend! You can do it! Onward you go!

Today Is Your Best Day

Focusing on the future, while a good strategy for plotting out a long-term course of action, does little to help with a momentary affliction, difficulty, or decision needing immediate action. Besides, you do not know the future, but *you do know one thing you can do today ... one step you can take … one action you can embrace.* You must live in the moment, take one day at a time, and walk your journey one step at a time. It is at those times that God bears your burdens, carries you, or opens amazing opportunities that defy the imaginable. He delivers you in powerful ways that define His holiness, splendor, and authority.

It has been said that many people spend their lifetime indefinitely preparing to live but forget to live! What a tragedy! The focus should be on today, not tomorrow. Getting organized is important; you would live in a state of pandemonium without planning. Those lists you make and adhere to on a daily and weekly basis prevent potential personal and professional train wrecks! But your energy should be given to living in the present. Your effort and activity should be focused on the events happening in the boardroom, the classroom, the living room … *today.* Tomorrow will present itself all too soon.

Scripture addresses this issue. In Matthew 6:34, Jesus teaches the multitude assembled, "Therefore do not worry about tomorrow, for tomorrow will worry about itself. Each day has enough trouble of its own."

Jesus recognizes the importance of celebrating each day and savoring it as a gift. You are alive today. God has given you this very day to enjoy His creation. Today you see your talents have impact. Today you encourage others and cherish your relationships. Today you fulfill your commitments. You don't know if you have the dawn of tomorrow.

Spending too much time living in the past is also wasting the precious hours of today.

It has been said that it is impossible to go to the next chapter when you keep rereading the last one. Move forward *today.* The past is behind you. What is done is done. You don't want to live forever in your past achievements. Nor do you want to live in the sadness, bitterness, or regret of your past failures or circumstances. Press onward.

"This is the day the LORD has made; let us rejoice and be glad in it" (Psalm 118:24) showcases that God has delivered you to live in victory *today*. He is not talking about yesterday or tomorrow but about giving thanks for *today*. Trust God for what He will do in your life *today*. Living in *today*, where daily life and the present converge, is where you are rooted. God directs your steps to move forward with confidence and peace. Recognize this day as a gift from the Lord by being fruitful, grateful, and courageous.

Trust God on the Distressing Days

In my darkest moments, I have clung to Jeremiah 29:11, which says, "'For I know the plans I have for you,' declares the LORD, 'plans to prosper you and not to harm you, plans to give you hope and a future.'"

That speaks to my heart! The God of the universe is saying He is in it to provide a way for you that is good. Yes, your circumstances could be miserable, but He has not forgotten you and has a plan. But you must trust in His purposes … day by day.

Christian writer and teacher R. Wayne Jackson says that even though God is not responsible for the evil acts and thoughts that a dark and fallen world perpetrates on others, He implements His sacred purposes in all these distressing matters and can ultimately turn adversity into victory. He can create progress and favorable results through the most adverse elements. Moreover, even the worst of these adverse elements do not frustrate God's divine plan for those who love Him.[4]

How encouraging! The challenge is that our dull spiritual eyesight might not be able to see the good that is now or that will be done. However, in God's perfect timing, it will be revealed. It will make sense. He is the God of restoration. Sometimes circumstances get worse before they get better. Perhaps those circumstances are needed to help you change the way you are acting and thinking. Perhaps they are being used to help other people who watch your response to your difficulties so that they, in turn, can be encouraged on how to respond to their present ordeals. Perhaps those circumstances are necessary for you to strengthen your faith, your temperament, or your compassion for others.

God's plan is to mend the broken. He will redeem a corrupt and dark world. He will repair relationships and restore peace. This process requires that He reconstruct hearts, attitudes, and beliefs. That can be painful, hard, and fatiguing, but that is the price of restoration. You must keep moving with the expectation that God will create beauty out of the ugly mess you might find yourself in right now. It is not too late.

Keep moving forward in great expectation to see what God is going to do in your life.

It could be radical. It could be transformational. Or it could be a tweak here and there. But God is up to something special for your benefit. Keep on running so you can get closer to see what that is! God is on the move too!

Be a Good Observer

Trusting in God may be a new concept or one that you have always believed but now question after a few bumps and many bruises on life's roller-coaster ride. You know in your heart that God has no rival. Yet your mind keeps throwing out doubts amid the brokenness, emptiness, and crises that you have experienced. That voice in your head keeps hurling accusations at God for abandoning you in your darkest hour. How can you trust a God like that?

Look at how other people did it. Pay attention! See what they did to persevere and survive. See how they were able to move one foot forward out of the quagmire they were in. No one is immune from the wounds of daily living.

Some people crumble when faced with hardship. The heaviness of their misery can be overwhelming, and they cannot get past it. They cannot let it go. They carry that grief with them day in and day out just like the mythological character Sisyphus, who is condemned to roll a great boulder to the top of a hill only to have it roll back down again. The myth contends that Sisyphus never gets relief from that heavy burden.

Some people retreat. But silence and isolation don't take the pain away. In fact, they only serve to increase the sense of loneliness, despair, and hopelessness.

Then there are the people who seem to bear well under great affliction and suffering. Pay attention to these mighty warriors who walk wounded on the battlefield of life. Their countenance remains joyful, their attitude is hopeful, and their faith seems strengthened even in the most difficult of circumstances. They seem to be the encouragers rather than the ones needing the pep talk! Watch these people! Observe how they have navigated their great trials in a healthy and authentic way. They may falter, but their faith and obedient trust in the One they serve never wavers.

If you do not have any role models like them in your direct sphere of influence, study other people who have walked through adversity with dignity, courage, and faith. They may be alive, or they may be deceased, but study their lives. Research their circumstances. How did they persevere? What did they do to battle the depression, anxiety, or chaos that can accompany hardship? How did they walk away from their circumstances in victory? Their habits and attitudes could transform the way you act and think in your trials. If they can exhibit grace, resiliency, and peace under fire, so can you!

Victory Is an Action Word!

You are on your way. You have moved forward recognizing the need to trust God for all things. You are moving at a pace that focuses on one day at a time being in the present rather than looking ahead to a future that can be elusive and irrelevant right now. You have observed or studied the lives of one or many good role models who have victoriously endured some rigorous hardships and have demonstrated tranquility, strength, and courage that you admire.

What next?

"Sometimes the great thing that heals us is doing a small thing again and again," said *New York Times* best-selling author and beloved blogger Ann Voskamp.[5]

In other words, doing at least one helpful, positive something each day. It could mean doing the same thing the next day … and the next day. Nike's iconic slogan "Just Do It" rings true. Just get out there and *do*. Planning each day deliberately with one or maybe a few activities will start the momentum back to healthy recovery. It can be a small thing that gets your battery charged and your feet moving forward. This is *not* a license to get overloaded.

However, being intentionally focused on doing *something* will automatically thrust you forward.

So what does that look like? Get out of bed. Make your bed. Prepare breakfast for the kids. Call your mom. Do sit-ups and jumping jacks. Read a proverb or psalm from the Bible. Get to work on time. Make that procrastinated client or personal call. Do a crossword puzzle. Give yourself a manicure. Take out the trash. Create a list with one thing that has made you joyful or that you are thankful for that day. Add to that list each day. Volunteer at the SPCA or the local children's hospital or any organization whose mission is important to you.

One insight. It is easy to get frustrated at the end of the day that you have not done all that you have intended on your to-do list. Again, start slowly. Do not overload that list. And, as importantly, at the end of the day, celebrate whatever you did accomplish rather than being discouraged over what was not done. It is important to have a sense of fulfillment at the end of the day rather than be exasperated over what is still left to do. Celebrate your achievements!

Have a Dream!

Have you dreamed big? What was it? No matter at what age you believed in your treasured and personal dream, it is a motivator to keep moving forward. Propelled by this dream, you can more nimbly put one foot in front of the other. Pursue your dream! If it has become a little fuzzy or perhaps buried under broken ambitions, hopes, or desires, resurrect it! God has given you talents to use and people to guide you in your pursuit. No dream is too big or too small. My friend, you can do it!

I want to encourage you with this story …

A ten-year-old Californian who was a promising tennis player once told a former British tennis champion that someday she was going to be the best tennis player in the world. That's a brash statement for a ten-year-old! When I was ten, I was trying to win at tetherball during school recess. But the precocious ten-year-old in my story was not backing down. The British champion, Mary Hardwicke Hare, knew this little girl had the talent. She knew this little girl had what it took to go the distance. But what she *didn't* know was if this little girl had the determination, discipline, and dedication to work hard enough to make her big dream happen.

That little girl made good on her promise. I know. She was my mother. From age ten until she was forced to retire at age nineteen because of a horseback riding accident, Maureen "Little Mo" Connolly was the top-ranked junior girl tennis player in the United States (1950), then the top-ranked woman tennis player in the United States (1951), and then the top-ranked woman tennis player in the world (1952–54). She won Wimbledon three years in a row (1952–54). In 1953, Little Mo was the first woman, and still the only American woman, to win the calendar Grand Slam (winning the Australian Open, French Open, Wimbledon, and US Open in one calendar year). She was inducted into the International Tennis Hall of Fame in 1968. But she didn't get to the top by just dreaming. She was fully dedicated to her craft and practiced with a tenacity and single-minded purpose to be the best at what she did.

In her book *Forehand Drive,* Mom wrote, "Any championship career has foundation stones. Mine were slavish work and driving determination."[6]

Dreams inspire everyone. Some people dream big. Others limit their dreams by their own doubt and hesitation. Sadly, many people dream and then don't back up their lofty aspirations with action. Nothing can be accomplished by just dreaming. All lofty ideas, grand goals, and creative thoughts are lifeless unless action is breathed into them.

How do you get your arms around your big dream? Here are a few steps: First, identify your dream. What is it? I know you have one! Maybe it has gotten lost over the years. Dig deeper. Think through the activities that speak to your heart—those things that get you excited! What do you like to do? What are you passionate about? What personal experiences or those of others have fueled a desire in you to make a difference? If you had to sum up your gifts, what do you think God has purposed you to do with them? What attributes do you believe God has entrusted into your care to impact others or to ignite a movement or to excel in a field? You don't need to be a world champion tennis player to live your dream.

Second, think of anything that will derail your dream. That can be an extensive list. What are your roadblocks to getting started? Financial limitations? Fear of failure? Too many things on your plate? Nobody to encourage you? On the surface, these all appear to be legitimate concerns. Now throw them out! Erase them! You are a child of God and not a slave to fear.

With God, all things are possible. If He created you to do something, you don't want to lose His ideal plan for you through excuses or people dragging you down. He has entrusted you with abilities to achieve your dream. Widen the circle of people around you who will encourage you, support you, share your vision, and catch you when you fall. If God created you for this, He did not call you into failure. If someone says you can't do something, don't let their negative words, actions, or thoughts detour you from the mighty dream that God has placed in your heart. Forgive them for their lack of faith in your dream and your ability to do it.

Do not let Satan distract you from your dream. Be very intentional about safeguarding your time to achieve your dream. Ask people to invest in your dream, hold you accountable, and pray for you. Remember, you will need others to walk alongside you to make this dream a reality.

Third, ask God to help you fulfill your dream. God has a great plan and purpose for you that you don't want to neglect or miss. If God gave you the gifts or skills or desire to do something, then He will walk with you, run with you, and carry you to accomplish that goal.

You cannot do this alone. God gave you the talents and desire. He will labor with you as you proceed forward to effectively and faithfully achieve your dream.

Ask God to show you favor as you press on toward your goal. Ask Him to reap a bountiful harvest through you. Ask Him for wisdom, stamina, and determination as you inch your way forward. Even though you will have some ease pursuing aspects of your dream because your talents will be in sync with what is required, the enemy will use challenges and barriers to stop you.

However, God has supplied you with what you need for the journey. You were born with these gifts. Keep to the road map, continue to put gas in your physical, emotional, and spiritual tank, and seek the face of God to navigate clearly. You will be held accountable for what you have done with the talents God has entrusted to you to achieve your dream. Friend, be encouraged that you have what it takes to live out that dream! Now go out and make it happen!

God Has Chosen You!

One last thing. Consider it an honor that God has chosen *you* with *this* dream for *this* season in time. It is unique. It is significant. It has your name on it. Most importantly, God knows you can do it! As a reminder, He will be tagging along with you every step of the way!

God has a sacred purpose for you. He is a God of action and has provided an opportunity for you to unleash your gifts and talents by wrapping your body, mind, and spirit around this dream. You will do more than just take up space in this big world. You will contribute to it!

You will make a difference! God expects nothing less of you.

And you will move forward. You can't make things happen by standing still or going backward! This dream is yours! Don't just walk with it! Run!

Pursue your dream. Envision it happening. Write out clearly how it will become a reality.

Acknowledge the disruptions, distractions, and difficulties that can get you stuck or leave you sidelined. Be strong and courageous. Focus on the goal. Let your passion guide you one step at a time, but keep your eyes on the Lord for balance, wisdom, and control. Steady and disciplined action, repeated again and again, will help you connect with the aspirations, ambitions, and anticipations that your dream requires. Savor this moment! Live now! Trust in the One who will always provide for you in His time and in His way. Onward you go, my friend!

What does momentum look like now? Glorious! You have a dream to pursue. You have a reason to pursue it. You have One who is walking with you to help you effectively, confidently, and successfully press on to achieve it! Be at peace!

Chapter Summary Points

- Taking time to recover and pause is fine for a season, but life beckons you to move forward.
- Beware of staying stuck on life's hold button.
  Life offers three directional options:
  - going backward
  - staying in place
  - moving forward
- Moving forward requires showing up, taking that first step, and staying in the game.
- Sometimes we must "do it scared" to move forward.
- Trust in God, His ways, and His timing always.
- Focus on today rather than on the past or the future.
- Call out Satan for who he is: a thug, a thief, and a liar who has no authority over you.
- Watch how other people have handled their hardships with victory.
- Celebrate your achievements each day rather than being disheartened over what has not been done.
- Identify your dream and the talents and passions you have been given to achieve it.
- Dream big, but give it to God.

Takeaway Question

What does your dream look like, how can you achieve it, and is there anything keeping you from pursuing it?

Applications: Six Ways You Can Move Forward

- Pray daily that God gives you the stamina, wisdom, and perseverance to do a few productive things each day.
  - Pray for those activities to increase daily and for your resolve to increase as well.
  - Denounce specifically any fearful, anxious, or discouraged thoughts that keep you from moving forward, and ask God to expel them from your heart and mind.
  - Record these prayers in a prayer journal so that you can refer to them daily, add to them, celebrate those that are answered, and pray over those that need attention.

- Call a friend and ask her/him to be your accountability partner to keep you energized and encouraged.
  - Choose a partner with whom you can be honest and transparent.
  - Check in with her/him regularly to discuss milestones met and roadblocks faced.

- Journal your feelings.
  - Focus on chronicling your range of heartfelt emotions.
  - Acknowledge the healing you are experiencing.
  - Use this journal as a pathway to communicate with God as you share these feelings with Him.

- Make a daily activity list and check off at least one activity completed on that list.
  - Celebrate your daily accomplishments.
  - Focus on what you achieved each day rather than on what you did not do.

- Within reason, add a new activity to the list and celebrate the completed victory.

- Throughout the day, give thanks to God for His provisions.
  - Think of one or more things daily that God has done for you and give Him thanks.
  - Remember how much God loves you even amid chaos and suffering.

- Identify your dream.
  - Define your dream specifically.
  - Understand and embrace why you are capable and most suitable with your gifts, talents, and passions to pursue this dream.
  - Identify the roadblocks in the way of accomplishing your dream.
  - Create a list of trusted people who will encourage you and help you achieve your dream.
  - Thank God for the specific talents He has given you to be best qualified to accomplish your dream.
  - Pray unceasingly for God's favor on this dream.

Forgetting what is behind and straining toward what
is ahead, I press on toward the goal to win the prize for
which God has called me heavenward in Christ Jesus.

(Philippians 3:13–14)

CHAPTER 2

RESTORING PERSEVERANCE

"God, Why Couldn't You Have?"

Carson Leslie was a stud—cool, brash, and confident. At fourteen, Carson was diagnosed with medulloblastoma, a mean brain cancer. Carson was a few years older than William. The boys went to The Covenant School, a classical Christian school that mightily rallied behind Carson and his wonderful family. We prayed. We helped. We prayed some more. Carson died at age seventeen in January 2010.

Carson was William's friend. Two years before Carson died, William was with him and his mom when they got the hospital's report saying Carson exhibited "no evidence of disease." Annette, Carson's dynamic, talented, and amazing mom, called me with this good news. I rejoiced all the way to their home to pick up William. After the hugs and excitement, William and I got in the car—William in the back seat, a little unusual. As we drove away, I asked, "William, aren't you thrilled Carson is doing so well?" No response. I asked again. No response. I looked back and saw William slouched over.

He shouted, "Why couldn't God have healed Daddy?" Authentic anger. Serious sadness. Great question.

Honestly, I think we all could fill in our own blank: "God, why couldn't You have_____?" Perhaps multiple times.

For some of you, that question has been resolved. Still others search for answers. And for some, that question has turned into an out-and-out fist-shaking battle cry against a perceived impotent, uncaring, and unjust God. Certainly a God in whom you refused to place either trust or allegiance. I couldn't argue with the depth of hurt William was feeling in that moment. His question seared my soul.

Reminder Alert: Suffering Is Part of Our Universal Experience

Suffering is a universal experience. God is quick to remind us of that in Scripture. That is our reality—yours and mine—until our last breath.

First Peter 4:12 reads, "Dear friends, do not be surprised at the painful trial you are suffering, as though something strange were happening to you." That fiery ordeal is predicted. It will happen. And it can be very painful. Some people seem to have more than their share of trials, but no one avoids a direct hit during a lifetime, usually multiple times. Pain starts at birth and continues from the ease, protection, and warmth of the womb into the difficult, vulnerable, and cold reality of life.

So count on it. When you least expect it. You won't go looking for trouble, but it sure comes looking for you. Misery is as much a part of life as joy. No one escapes the wounds caused by suffering. Ecclesiastes 3:1, 4 says, "There is a time for everything, and a season for every activity under heaven … a time to weep and a time to laugh, a time to mourn and a time to dance."

Agony lives alongside gladness in this life. You are not immune from suffering's grasp.

Nor is anyone else you know.

What Does God Say to Do?

God does not tell you to crawl into a hole, run away, or fake happiness. Pretending nothing is happening is a lie. God is authentic and asks you to be the same. Call out the enemy. Stand your ground. Do not be shaken. God instructs us to persevere. As 1 Peter 5:8 says, "Be self-controlled and alert. Your enemy the devil prowls around like a roaring lion looking for someone to devour." But Peter continues in verse 9: "Resist him, standing firm in the faith, because you know that your brothers throughout the world are undergoing the same kind of sufferings."

What a message! Stay disciplined, vigilant, and faithful. God reminds you that you belong to a fellowship of others who are suffering. This misery is endured by people in every corner of the globe at all times.

Carson's favorite Bible verse was Joshua 1:9: "Have I not commanded you? Be strong and courageous. Do not be terrified; do not be discouraged, for the LORD your God will be with you wherever you go."

God calls you to be His warrior. He tells you to continue the fight. He doesn't expect you to back down in fear or hopelessness. He doesn't signal you to retreat. God tells you to *persevere.* That is a command. God gives this directive because He will be with you every step of the way … wherever you go.

Until his last breath, Carson held firm to that verse. He persevered because God demanded him to do so. Even when he knew he was never going to graduate from high school, get married, or have kids. That's a tough reality for a teenager to handle. But Carson persevered in a courageous way that so rocked those around him that Covenant's gymnasium bears his name. He met with and inspired some of the biggest names in sports, entertainment, and politics and wrote a popular book. All before he was eighteen! Carson persevered because God says we should. God calls you to do the same. Persevere.

God Has Got This!

You and I persevere because God says we should, but He puts muscle behind that request rather than just telling us to do it without a reason.

He has a plan and a purpose in this suffering. He gets it. He is our provider. Our safety net. Our refuge. God knows when life throws you painful, numbing, and flat-out debilitating zingers and how those direct hits sting like crazy.

He knew that your job would end before you even took it.

He knew the restless heart of your unfaithful partner since eternity past.

He knew about that Alzheimer's diagnosis before your mother received it—actually, before she was even born.

Nothing surprises God. He has a good plan and purpose for you—despite yourself and despite your circumstances.

God's ways and your ways are not always aligned. Many times, they feel like they're in opposition to each other. Isaiah 55:8–9 says, "'For my thoughts are not your thoughts, neither are your ways my ways,' declares the Lord. 'As the heavens are higher than the earth, so are my ways higher than your ways and my thoughts than your thoughts.'"

He is God! Just because something looks bad to you doesn't mean it looks bad to our sovereign Lord. You only see in part. In fact, what you think is terrible at the time may seem glorious to God. Conversely, things that look good to you may not look so good to Him. God could be protecting you from your desires and pursuits because they could be so much less than what He purposes for you. Or, even worse, chasing after them could destroy you.

God is the only One with the full perspective on any situation. He perceives all with a heart of love, compassion, and redemption. He sees. He knows. Nothing is wasted, as He uses it for your good. Your suffering is not in vain. That is why He can be trusted. That is why He commands you to persevere. In His loving-kindness, He will provide the way out in His time.

The Lord is power in your time of weakness and says in 2 Corinthians 12:9, "My grace is sufficient for you, for my power is made perfect in weakness." His power is magnified as it lifts you up and propels you forward when your own strength, energy, and motivation are depleted. It is then that God's strength radiates through you. At that fragile moment, God works in your life to redeem and rescue you. Your hardship, brokenness, and suffering provide the ideal backdrop for the display of divine power. What an encouragement to you and others!

God has a specifically designed plan for you. Whether you can accomplish it with both feet on the ground or whether God must carry you to get after it, His ultimate purpose for you is good—really good—even if your prognosis is grim, your circumstances look bleak, and your resources are gone. Trust that God has got this! Don't give up! Persevere with confidence!

Don't Forget to Remember

You only must look a little into your history to see how God has rescued you. Don't forget to remember how He has either physically, spiritually, or emotionally pulled you from what could have been your wreckage. Perhaps it won't be until the other side of heaven that you will see how God mercifully delivered you from disaster. Be grateful that God overcomes your suffering with His protection, mercy, and love.

When I was six, I had a serious horseback riding accident. Our excitable dog accidentally bit the horse I was riding on his fetlock (the joint above the horse's ankle). My horse reared up, I slipped off his back beneath him, and he stepped on my face! While I don't have a horseshoe permanently implanted on my face, I have scars from the plastic surgery that immediately followed. (To add some drama to this incident, on the way to the hospital, my speeding ambulance crashed—but that's another story!) If my horse had stepped inches higher, I could have been blinded for life or my skull could have been crushed.

A few years ago, I was driving back to Dallas from an event a few hours away. After checking my side mirror, I changed lanes. Out of nowhere, a car raced into my changing lane, causing me to jerk the wheel back into my lane. Too much of a jerk caused my SUV to hit the guardrail and spin out of control in acrobatic circles over four lanes on one of the busiest highways in Texas! I imagine the angels in heaven were cheering wildly as God so nimbly pulled my SUV safely to a halt on the highway without one scratch on me or another car.

Only after my stalled car was pushed over to the shoulder by four people, and I watched semitrailer trucks and big rigs go whizzing by, did I realize how easily I could have been pulverized. The tow truck driver hauling my stalled car and me back to Dallas told me that a few days earlier he had been summoned to an accident with the same situation as I had just experienced, only that SUV had flipped over multiple times.

That story, he said very sadly with a hushed tone, had not ended well.

Perhaps you have experienced trials that have tested your faith, stamina, and patience.

Maybe you've questioned God's whereabouts as you felt pummeled by circumstances—resulting from either your own decisions or through no fault of your own. Perhaps you're there right now. Do not forget to remember the times that God has carried you, protected you, and saved you from peril.

You still might have gotten hurt physically, emotionally, or spiritually, but you ultimately emerged stronger from it. Or maybe the fact you survived at all is credited to the miraculous intervention and abundant grace of God watching over you. Don't forget that God, who loves beyond measure, will rescue you again no matter what your circumstances are right now. And He will do it again later. And again.

Think about it. You are here on this side of heaven to be used by God. You have been rescued for a mighty purpose, my friend!

You Don't Know Who's Watching!

When you are in dark places, people are watching. Yes, you can almost feel eyeballs on your back. When you are on top of the world, I suppose people watch too. But all things that go up must come down, and it is only a matter of time before something goes down. Unravels. Implodes. Destructs. Or all the above simultaneously. Do you succumb to defeat and despair? Or do you rise to the occasion with a commitment to overcome and persevere? Life's measurement of success is not by counting our days but by making our days count—even in those desert experiences.

In the message of hope given to the prophet Ezekiel in the valley of dry bones, God breathed His breath into the very decimated bones of the slain Israelites strewn all over the battlefield plain and brought them back to life. Ezekiel 37:5–6 says, "This is what the Sovereign LORD says to these bones: 'I will make breath enter you, and you will come to life. ... Then you will know that I am the LORD.'"

So, too, God infuses His breath into your lifelessness and brokenness. You are emotionally, physically, and spiritually resuscitated. People see what faithful trust really looks like when you are in those desert experiences. You rally from a dead person walking—scorched and bloodied from life's battle wounds—to one who has renewed strength because of your hope in the Lord. Your dedication to Christ is magnified as those around you observe peace, calm, and even joy radiating through your affliction. A watching world sees Jesus's transforming power in you. Your suffering becomes your platform to showcase His grace and strength in you.

Matthew 5:16 reminds us that eyes are watching: "Let your light shine before men, that they may see your good deeds and praise your Father in heaven." People are walking witnesses when suffering invades their lives. They inspire others to move forward. To release anger. To forgive others ... and themselves. Their ability to persevere despite their circumstances ignites hope in a world that is breathlessly watching.

Hope is what helps you dodge those curveballs or catch them. Without hope, you are bruised to the core. How people marvel when you can be hit and yet shake it off. Sometimes you hobble. Sometimes you run. *But you are moving forward.* And as your legs are churning, you are encouraging others in the process who are stuck on hold, have decided to quit, or think their life does not matter.

When you persevere, you offer no greater testimony of God's abundant grace and loving-kindness. Some people can praise God amid their suffering; others can't. Some people can make sense of it; others can't. It might be that you can't see the power of overcoming the ugly until you look back later. Then you can understand more clearly Jesus's presence as He has walked every step with you in the mayhem, darkness, and difficulty. He has been your protector and provider even if you can't see it right now. The point is you got through it. You persevered.

You declared victory rather than surrendered to defeat. People will always be watching.

Give God Your Full Attention

C. S. Lewis exposes the enemy's evil strategy to trip us up. In his brilliantly clever *The Screwtape Letters*, Lewis showcases the logic of Screwtape, the senior devil who is teaching his "young fiend" and nephew, Wormwood, the art of all things diabolical. He gleefully acknowledges that dull, discouraging, and dreary years are the enemy's tools to extinguish a vibrant faith and joyful life.

Screwtape gloats to Wormwood: "You see, it is so hard for these creatures to *persevere*. The routine of adversity, the gradual decay of youthful loves and youthful hopes, the quiet despair (hardly felt as pain) of ever overcoming the chronic temptations with which we have again and again defeated them, the drabness which we create in their lives, and the inarticulate resentment with which we teach them to respond to it—all this provides admirable opportunities of wearing out a soul by attrition."[7]

Screwtape rejoices that assaults of endless hardships, lost loves, and dwindling passions cause a gradual erosion of hope among humans. He relishes their misery when they recognize their inability to resist recurring temptations. How Screwtape delights in the discontentment of their lives that, ultimately, exhaust their soul, implode their persistence, and quench their spirit.

Indeed, the enemy wears down perseverance through years of difficulties, despair, and disappointments. Crushed dreams, repeated missteps, and broken relationships make you want to bail. "I am done!" you say as you defiantly turn your back, heart, and mind against God. His apparent indifference to your continued defeats just gets you deeper into the quagmire of sin, depression, and hopelessness. It's tough to hang on when your legs are dangling over the edge of a cliff and the dark abyss below just seems ready to swallow you up. Sometimes you just want to let go...

Friends, never let moments of desperation—when the bumps and bruises of daily living come crashing into your home and heart—determine your feelings about God.

Do not establish what you think about God in a crisis. Do not judge the Almighty Creator when chaos is coming at you like a freight train. Do not launch your faith as the by-product of your circumstances. God is still loving, kind, and good even when your circumstances are not. The breadth of God's character, mercy, and grace does not change when adversity tackles you.

Instead, back up. Quiet your thoughts. Chill for a time.

You are not immune from suffering. That 100% guarantee comes the moment you emerge from the womb. But God also guarantees He will walk with you through it and, most incredibly, will use it to bless you. The situations that seem to compromise your future can also be powerful tools God uses to mold you, mature you, and strengthen you. Wait until the frenzied pace slows down. The chaotic confusion simmers down. The maddening disruptions settle down. Do not let messy circumstances determine your theology.

God deserves your full attention. Throughout the Bible, God repeatedly tells you that nothing can separate you from His love, and because of this, He will never forget, leave, or forsake you. Isaiah 49:16 says that the God of the universe has your name engraved on the palms of His hands.

It's incredibly hard, if not impossible, to grab onto the depth of those astounding words when you are at the end of yourself. Let it sink into your soul that our holy, perfect, and all-knowing God has your very name etched on His hands. The One who created you sees you. He loves you. He remembers you. He deserves your full consideration over quieter times rather than your condemning judgment when storms are dumping their full fury on your world.

Take time to get to know God when the waters are calmer. He is ready now!

Celebrate Your Discomfort!

Trials are God's rescue specialty. You can take that to the bank. The Greek word for "trials" is *peirasmos* and means things that test our faith in and obedience to God. Simply stated, trials test our consistency of faith. James 1:2–4 says, "Consider it pure joy, my brothers, whenever you face trials of many kinds, because you know that the testing of your faith develops perseverance. Perseverance must finish its work so that you may be mature and complete, not lacking anything."

James purposefully uses the word *perseverance*—the very dynamic that the old demon Screwtape seeks to weaken. Perseverance is stamina on steroids. Going the distance ultimately results in spiritual maturity and steadfast faithfulness to God.

The victory is enduring the trial rather than succumbing to it. Finishing rather than quitting. Standing firm, fearless, and strong in the midst of hardship to emerge undaunted on the other side. The triumph is in pressing forward rather than letting the trial defeat you.

Perseverance, by its very nature, requires patience. What, then, produces patience?

Discomfort produces patience. Working through hurtful challenges and hardships. Reconciling the relationships that have gone astray and have caused you pain. Defying the enemy who wants you to fail.

By declaring, "I don't want my identity to be my grief, my anger, my bitterness," and by asserting, "I don't want to live like this anymore," you are now confidently stating that no matter how long it takes to get done, you are going to be patient in seeing it through. No matter the number of detours, derailments, or dead ends, you will persevere.

Thinking this backward, discomfort produces patience that gives you the perseverance (endurance) needed for a life of spiritual maturity and faithfulness. God recalibrates the distress Satan intended for destruction to be used for your good. God wants you to live in the fullness of His purpose with complete contentment—and that includes having the perseverance to bear the hardships you have encountered.

James 1:12 has a good word for those who persevere: "Blessed is the man who perseveres under trial, because when he has stood the test, he will receive the crown of life that God has promised to those who love him."

Remember this blessing—that those who persevere by fully trusting in and loving God will be given a glorious reward. Those who have staying power will pass the finish line and collect the prize. This steadfast endurance will be honored by spending eternity in heaven.

God's Love Is Enough

Have you ever felt God wasn't listening to you? That He was unaware that your heart was splintering like a log exploding under the heat of a winter's fire? Wondering if He really cares? The enemy is on the assault, and you feel like you have a big bull's-eye on your back. Maybe things are even getting worse before they are getting better. It's easy to have lapses in belief during those times when you feel like God is not enough.

Have you ever felt like that? It is a lonely, painful place to live.

I get it! But I want to answer those questions. God is enough! *He is everything*! And because of that, my friend, you can hope in Him. Even when you can't see things working out, God is who He says He is. This is what God says about Himself related to His love for you:

> I have loved you with an everlasting love; I have drawn you with loving-kindness. (Jeremiah 31:3)

> So do not fear, for I am with you; do not be dismayed, for I am your God. I will strengthen you and help you; I will uphold you with my righteous right hand. (Isaiah 41:10)

> Never will I leave you; never will I forsake you. (Hebrews 13:5)

First Peter 5:7 instructs, "Cast all your anxiety on him because he cares for you."

First John 4:8 even goes so far as to say, "Whoever does not love does not know God, because God is love."

Everything that *is* has only happened because God has allowed it to happen. Every talent you have, every success you have experienced, and every joy that makes you squeal happens because of God's love for you.

Conversely, while God does not delight in the diseases, tragedies, and heartaches that befall humanity (that disgrace belongs to Satan), He knows all and allows all to coexist in a world tainted with the darkness of sin. But He takes what the enemy wants to use for evil and uses it for the good of humans. His purpose for your life will ultimately prevail in ways unknown right now but will be used for your future benefit. Count on that!

God's abundant love is steadfast even in your season of hardship and sorrow. Don't forget to remember what God has done for you in the past. Though you might be stuck at an impasse right now, God knows. More importantly, God's love for you is enough to handle it!

He's got this! Persevere, my friend!

Trusting God's Love Produces Hope

God's Word says in 2 Corinthians 4:16–18, "Therefore we do not lose heart. Though outwardly we are wasting away, yet inwardly we are being renewed day by day. For our light and momentary troubles are achieving for us an eternal glory that far outweighs them all. So we fix our eyes not on what is seen, but on what is unseen. For what is seen is temporary, but what is unseen is eternal."

Just because you can't see the good right now doesn't mean it isn't happening or won't happen in the future. Yes, your unhinged circumstances might be staring you in the face. They can be painful, worrisome, and exhausting. However, Scripture says they are "momentary."

What propels you forward is trusting God. Your unseen realities are no less real because you cannot see them at this particular moment. God's plans for you on this side of heaven and in eternity with Him produce a glory far grander than these current miseries. It gives you reason to praise God for what He is doing even when you cannot see it.

Ephesians 3:20–21 speaks to the bigness of God's plan for you: "Now to him who is able to do immeasurably more than all we ask or imagine, according to his power that is at work with us, to him be the glory."

Putting your trust in God produces the joy of hope because His plans are exceedingly more than you can ask or think. This hope (an absolute certainty and confidence that God works on your behalf for your intended good) prevents worry and angst. It provides security, alertness, and peace that God does not err and that your future is safely protected in His hands. Such hope prevents overreacting and getting overwhelmed with what you see in your present circumstances. You can control your responses by choosing where you place your hope.

Trust and hope are essential travel buddies on life's journey. However, hope traveling solo without trust is only a wish, which is nothing more than a longing, craving, or yearning. A wish can be fleeting, temporary, and short-lived—if even acted on at all.

However, hope and trust are anchored in faith. Hebrews 11:1 gives us a working definition of faith: "Now faith is being sure of what we hope for and certain of what we do not see."

The Bible says that faith is confident about an outcome (what we hope for) before it is yet to happen. It is trusting in the promises of God even in your season of suffering. Faith crushes any doubt that God is who He says He is. Faith is persevering in the pursuit of your goals with the calm assurance that what you hope for will be yours. It is believing your aspirations are right, just, and worthy even if you will never see the outcome on this side of heaven. You wait with confidence, knowing the ultimate prize—eternal life and the realities of heaven—are secured through your faith.

Trusting God's love, watchfulness, and care for you produces an unshakable and confident expectation that He will do what He says and deliver. Even if you are not able to see it right now, your faith in that promise propels you forward in anticipation of future blessings. Armed with your trust and hope, onward you go!

Pruning Leads to Progress

So we recognize we need to give God a fair shake. He needs our full attention. We do not make decisions about His love and provision in the middle of the hurricane. And we do not react when we are amid those cyclones by diminishing or limiting our perception of God.

The Bible also convinces us that He has full authority over heaven, earth, and the depths. We see the beauty of God's creation that declares His holy existence. Breathtaking cloud formations and sunsets, the sweet fragrances of roses and honeysuckle, and the grace of an agile hummingbird or galloping cheetah showcase a mighty God who is powerful, artistic, and creative. We marvel at the splendor of nature He fashions for our enjoyment and that reveals the reality of His presence.

But maybe you just need a little more convincing. Maybe your faith needs a little straightening after a few failures or sorrows have twisted your belief. Maybe you are fearful of change. Or maybe the enemy has you firmly grasped in a headlock, and you need to silence those perverse voices in your head.

Gardeners know that luscious vines of grapes are only produced when they are first cut down to the stalk. Such pruning of vines takes time—sometimes a few years—but the ultimate product will be healthy, abundant, and delicious fruit.

Don't forget to remember how God's pruning blesses you for your own good. As the Master Gardener, He snips, trims, and clips areas of your life that are destructive, hurtful, and unpleasant to you and to others. After all, God knows everything about you. Psalm 139:1–3 reminds us of this: "O LORD, you have searched me and you know me. You know when I sit and when I rise; you perceive my thoughts from afar. You discern my going out and my lying down; you are familiar with all my ways."

You can't surprise God. Yet God doesn't want you to be stuck, scared, and unable to live a fruitful and joyful life. So He must cut off parts of your life that are preventing you from loving and living well. On your own, even with your best intentions, you can make huge messes of your relationships, decisions, and actions. God knows the only way to get you back on track is to cut out the dead and rotted debris from your life.

You are being pruned daily. So am I. In marriages, God peels away those things that aggravate each other. He wants children to exchange bad habits for good ones. He wants you to make better choices, rid yourself of destructive behavior, and feed yourself with healthier things.

As in the process of gardening, God's pruning sometimes looks destructive in all He cuts away.

However, He knows the final product will be a richness of life and a greater harvest of fruit. What hurts deeply at the time will yield greater abundance.

Trials Can Be Treasures in Disguise

So, too, trials refine you. The same is true of the perfume frankincense. All the magnificent qualities of frankincense's fragrance, like so many other perfumes, resins, and oils, arise only after being heated in the flame. Similarly, adversity burns away habits clouding your focus and harming your relationships, recalibrating your attention to important, life-giving action. Your heart is purified in the process.

Suffering can awaken in you deeper feelings about people, generating or strengthening empathy and sensitivity. It can create understanding and tolerance where once criticism, harshness, and hatred resided. Suffering can generate new life missions to better the world. So many significant causes were established from heartache and, out of that pain, a desire to make the world safer, healthier, and kinder. Great progress has been made in medicine, the environment, the arts, and ministry because broken people were stirred into action on a path paved with grief.

As my William says, "The loss of my father gives me the ability to truly empathize with and encourage a wide array of individuals who have experienced similar loss."

Joni Eareckson Tada is the inspiring Christian quadriplegic author, radio host, and founder of Joni and Friends, a worldwide ministry dedicated to the disabled community. She was paralyzed in 1967 at age seventeen after diving into shallow water. Over fifty-five years, Joni has been bound to a wheelchair. For most people, that would be absolutely devastating, particularly if that accident happened as a teenager with so many dreams and adventures yet to conquer. Joni's steadfast faith, perseverance, and trust in a holy and perfect God enabled her to establish a ministry that has delivered wheelchairs, advocacy for the disabled, and the hope of the Gospel to millions of people since its founding in 1979.

Joni said to the Lord, "Jesus, do you see that wheelchair? You were right when you said that in this world we would have trouble, because that thing was a lot of trouble. But the weaker I was in that thing, the harder I leaned on you. And the harder I leaned on you, the stronger I discovered you to be. It never would have happened had you not given me the bruising of the blessing of that wheelchair."[8]

Joni was restored, even though she has never walked again. That wheelchair became the pivot point for her healing. It was through her weakness that God's power showed up and has continued to heal her brokenness with all its messiness. Through Joni's suffering, she became God's mighty messenger for the disabled in advocating for their needs and inspiring them with the hope found in Jesus to lift them from their despair. God used Joni's wheelchair to remind her daily that He was the One pushing it.

And So …

Suffering is no respecter of ethnicity, age, gender, socioeconomic status, or profession. It is an equal opportunity invader. We also see trials have an upside. We know many times the greatest breakthroughs sprout from torched lives. Many blessings are only received from the residue of pain, and the path of suffering is the only way to attain them. Perhaps you still need to be convinced.

When you persevere through trials …

- Strength and courage replace weakness and complacency.
- Wisdom and maturity oust timidity and passiveness.
- Confidence is regained.
- Recklessness becomes responsibility.
- Self-absorption dies to servant leadership.
- Perversity gives way to discipline.
- Appreciation and gratitude are profoundly increased.
- Relationships are reconciled.
- The prodigal returns.
- Love and compassion break through the barriers of hate and intolerance.
- Great movements are begun that help humanity and the underserved.

- Heroes emerge.
- True, authentic intimacy with God is experienced.
- Hope is restored.
- God is glorified.

Many trials fix what is broken, find what is lost, and generate love for the unlovable.

Trials force you to break through your fears, anxieties, and doubts and stand strong, confident, and empowered. Your arrogance implodes as you are stripped of everything, and a sweet humility emerges in its place. You recognize that the praise of humans is seductive and popularity is fickle as status fluctuates and possessions diminish.

How comforting to focus on an audience of One, for God's love never wavers. The Bible consistently praises His commitment to never forsake or leave His children. You are forever changed when roadblocks make you stumble, and you get back up all the better for it. The fire refines you to forgive, love, and serve rather than blame, resent, and abuse. Trials draw humanity closer to God. You see His abiding love when you are weak and weary because His presence directs your steps or even carries you when you can't move forward.

As English writer, journalist, philosopher, and art critic G. K. Chesterton said, "One sees great things from the valley; only small things from the peak."[9]

Embrace Those Trials

William's dad was called Home when William was nine. His buddy Carson Leslie was called Home when William was fourteen. He was hit with two big losses in five years. Tough for a preteen-turned-teenager to grasp. But William also understood that God loves him and can be fully trusted.

The enemy had delivered some fierce blows to William, so he knew at an early age that life could be hard, unfair, and devastating. But William also knew God had a plan through all this that never diminished His goodness, kindness, and everlasting love.

"My questioning of my father's death did not end when I was nine. I continued asking this question even in college. I recognize I will never be able to fully answer this question, and there is nothing wrong with that. However, I believe God recognizes our pain and mourns with us. He is not some abstract being detached from our suffering. He loves us unconditionally and is always with us. Most importantly, He has a redemptive plan for us through His Son, Jesus Christ, and my faith is securely placed in Christ. God is who He says He is, and I trust Him completely."

William got to that good place with God because his trials tested his faith, and he had to reckon where he stood with the Almighty. William had to come face-to-face with the God of the universe and acknowledge whether He could be trusted or not. That meant when he wept at his father's gravesite and felt the loss of his good friend Carson. Even now, years later, he must remind himself of God's trustworthiness when his heart hurts, or he sees man's inhumanity to man, or he feels disappointed or uncertain about something.

William had some difficult dialogues with God. As he says, "I had conversations with God that ended in my tears and a healthy outpouring of emotion." But they were honest because they came from a broken and confused heart. God can take it! He wants our authenticity even if it is accusatory, tearful, or perplexed. He wants a two-way communication. God cherishes time with you. Lay out your grievances to Him. Be patient to hear Him speak and to allow Him to respond. He can take whatever you bring Him. God wants a relationship with you.

William understands the treasure of those trials because they solidified his certainty that God is faithful and can always be trusted. William knows God has his back, and His love is enduring. William does not forget to remember all that God has done for him in the past and all that He is doing for him now. He also has great confidence God will continue His goodness into the future. William's firm faith in his Savior propels him to move forward with confidence. Life will still throw him curveballs, loved ones will still die, and failures will still happen, but William knows he will persevere.

My friend, you can too!

Chapter Summary Points

- Suffering is a universal experience.
- Do not establish what you think about God in a crisis.
- People are watching how you persevere in crisis.
- Give God your full attention.
- Trials test the consistency of your faith.
- Discomfort triggers the pathway to perseverance.
- Weakness provides the perfect setting for the display of divine power.
- Don't forget to remember how God has provided for you … and will do so again!
- Trusting in God produces a confident hope anchored on the assurance that His plans for you are good.
- Trials can be treasures in disguise.
- God wants a personal, deep, and authentic relationship with you.

Takeaway Question

What circumstances, fears, or lies from the enemy are keeping you from persevering in your relationship with God?

Applications: Eight Ways You Can Strengthen Your Perseverance

- Don't forget to remember how God has rescued you from other difficult or compromising circumstances in the past and that He can do it again.
  - Record the times that you know you have been rescued by God from ruin, harm, and even death.
  - Identify specific issues right now in your afflictions and ask God's mercy, grace, and provision to overcome them.

- Pray daily for patience and stamina as you confront discouragements, discomforts, and hardships of any kind.
  - Find the best time to ask God for His strength and clarity, to confess your insecurities, to discuss your grievances, to ask for forgiveness, and to thank Him for His kindnesses to you.
  - God wants time with you.
  - He can take whatever you bring Him!

- Call your accountability partner, friend, mentor, or community group members to encourage you when you are struggling and feel like throwing in the towel.

- Recognize trials as a blessing to expose your weaknesses, reveal God's power, and draw you closer to Him.
  - Chronicle each past trial and how you experienced God's grace to overcome it.
  - Chronicle how you have grown through each trial.
  - Chronicle the positive outcomes of each trial.
  - Chronicle your thankfulness.

- Record the ways God has carried you through each day and how much that demonstrates God's love for you in providing for your needs in each situation.

- Chronicle each step of how you overcame an obstacle and make notes where you had lapses of belief in God's ability to resolve the issue as well as times when you fully trusted in God's provision.
  - Study carefully the ways God directed your steps to victory to utilize them in the future.
  - Be aware of the consistent strongholds the enemy has on your fragility so that you may recognize them more easily in your next struggle and be able to either persevere through them or prevent them altogether.

- Memorize Scripture for immediate recall to strengthen your perseverance when you are stymied in fear or stuck in hopelessness.

- Share your experience with others of how you persevered and tackled your trial, because they will be watching and will be empowered by your story.
  - Tell it over dinner, over coffee, at work, at church, in your book club, watching your kid's baseball game … *anywhere*!
  - Blog it.
  - Post it on Facebook and Instagram.
  - Text it, email it, Twitter it.
  - You have no idea how much that can encourage someone.

We also rejoice in our sufferings, because we know
that suffering produces perseverance; perseverance,
character; and character, hope.

(Romans 5:3–4)

CHAPTER 3

RESTORING JOY

Cheerful Confidence

"Joy is the cheerful confidence in God's power to deliver." William shared this with me, and I love it! God *does* deliver! Trusting in Him gives you the peace, confidence, and comfort to move forward even when your circumstances seem to betray you. You don't just move forward; you move forward with unbridled joy!

Now, I did not do somersaults and sing from the mountaintops when my beloved Bob lost his battle with cancer. You don't jump for joy when natural disasters or pandemics announce themselves with massive destruction, when man's inhumanity to man is revealed, or when hatred claims casualties. Those are dark days. Pain will always be part of life's experience because you and I live in a fallen world. However, even amid such chaos, horror, and suffering, joy can be planted to bear fruit. But that is possible only if you have the belief, the conviction, and *the confidence* that God *always* wins.

Does that seem impossible? How can you be cheerful when everything, absolutely everything, around you is crumbling? It's especially hard to be joyful when life is hitting you with two-by-fours. It hurts to just breathe! Laughter has no room in a hopeless soul. Since Scripture says in James 1:2,

"Consider it pure joy, my brothers, whenever you face trials of many kinds," then God *must* have a plan to back that up.

Healing Takes Time

Let's be honest. Wounds don't heal overnight. Recovery can take a lifetime. Or maybe it never fully happens on this side of heaven. Tragedy comes in all shapes and sizes. Disease, pandemics, abuse, divorce, and other grueling lifestyle reversals can immediately bring you to your knees and change your world in a nanosecond. Loss can seize your soul and splinter it into a thousand pieces at a moment's notice. Sorrow can carve a hole in your anguished heart no echocardiogram will ever detect.

Immediately after Bob breathed his last breath, I remember hearing people laughing outside the hospital's ICU halls. I thought, *How can they laugh? My world has just been turned upside down! How can anyone feel joy and celebration at this moment?* Then, minutes later, I looked out the hospital window and saw Dallas's traffic moving briskly on a crowded expressway. In disbelief, I almost screamed, "How can people be going anywhere? How can the world keep spinning when my world has just stopped so abruptly?"

For a moment, I was totally bewildered at the thought of the world moving forward while mine had just imploded. It was like someone had come from behind and hit me so hard I could not breathe! What would tomorrow look like without Bob in it? Despite our three-year cancer journey, with all the "grim" prognoses and "terminal" taglines, I simply was not ready to let Bob go.

A New Normal

In 1979, freshly graduated from the University of Virginia, I came back to Dallas. I had an excellent job as membership director / special events coordinator at Willow Bend Polo and Hunt Club in West Plano. At the time, there were few houses in the area and only a two-lane country road to get to the club. Willow Bend was originally a country club for people who liked to ride horses and swim. There were polo matches every Sunday. Tennis courts and a racquetball/fitness center were later added to give the club some modern appeal for nonriders.

It was there that I made good on a goal I had been harboring for over ten years—to crusade against the cancer that had taken Mom from our family and claimed her life so prematurely at age thirty-four. In 1980, I organized some fun events for the Willow Bend members over a weekend, including a horse show, a bake sale, a tennis tournament, collecting pledges for lengths swum, and a dance marathon. This new fundraiser was called A Weekend at Willow Bend to Wipe Out Cancer. That first year, we raised $6,000 for the American Cancer Society. The next year, we added a casual country-themed party in one of the large indoor riding rings at Willow Bend and raised $15,000. From there, many events and fundraising initiatives were added, and sponsors were secured. The name was changed to Wipe Out Kids' Cancer (WOKC), and the fundraiser was officially established as a nonprofit organization in 1983. A movement began.

For decades now, WOKC has raised and funded millions of dollars for innovative and novel pediatric cancer research projects all over the country. Additionally, WOKC has established social engagement and emotional support programs that provide hope and comfort to these heroic children with cancer and their resilient families—"medicine for the soul" as parents have described. I have met thousands of young, courageous cancer warriors through our charitable organization who have claimed victory over this scourge of a pediatric disease. But sadly, we have lost some of our valiant heroes fighting this disease. Immediately following a funeral I attended, a grieving mother said to me, "I don't know how I am going to cope with this new normal." She was assessing how her life could move one step forward with someone so very special now missing.

I get it. How do you live a new normal? How do you remain whole when your body has been battered by grief? When your heart has been ruthlessly ripped out of your chest? When your mind is in a state of confusion and fogginess? You can't see clearly. And your soul, that intangible, deep, and most ethereal part of your being, feels buried with your loved one. No matter the circumstance, this new normal is inconceivable. You want your old usual back! Change is always hard, but this new dynamic totally implodes your life. How do you deal with a new normal that is such a devastating game changer? How do you collect yourself to be whole again when you feel shredded—mind, body, and soul? How can you ever feel joy again? Let's look to God for the answers.

What Does God Say to Do?

God understands your broken heart. He knows the depth of a mother's grief in burying her child. He knows the pain of betrayal and the infuriation when justice is being corrupted. He knows the frailty of the human condition. But the Bible says that His will for you is to "be joyful always; pray continually; give thanks in all circumstances, for this is God's will for you in Christ Jesus" (1 Thessalonians 5:16–18). That can seem a little extreme when your life seems to be careening out of control. You can't imagine getting your arms around this mess, your mind around this chaos, and your heart around this pain—much less feeling joyful about it. *What was God thinking?*

God is telling you to be joyful. It can seem impracticable and, quite frankly, impossible, but God asks you to do this because it glorifies Him and is for your good. Proverbs 15:13 says, "A happy heart makes the face cheerful, but heartache crushes the spirit." God knows the state of your heart will govern everything about your life. He also knows that joy is not predicated on circumstances but on a relationship with Him.

Yes, God knows there is a time to mourn, grieve, and cry. Life is hard with tragic and sad circumstances invading your personal space. God knows everything happening in your life—the victories and defeats, the delights and sorrows. But when life delivers either blessings or crushing blows, your joy is not to be tethered to any of it but, rather, to trust that God has a plan and purpose in all things that will be good for you.

God knows the extent of your humanness. He knows you are prone to wander. Whether it is straying from the things that you know you should do and, instead, doing the things you know you shouldn't be doing. Whether it is defiantly rebelling against authority. Human nature can get you in all sorts of pickles. God knows that. He knows your every move before you even take that first step or think that first thought. So God knows that your intentional actions or those things out of your control can rob you of your joy. Yet God still calls you to be joyful. He expects that from you and from me … and from all of humanity.

So in obedience to God, you are called to choose joy, despite yourself or despite your circumstances. Even if a new normal takes you to the end of yourself. That's a tall order, but if God requests it, He must have a way to get it done.

The Grief of the Unexpected

Let's back up. Honestly, the last thing I felt after Bob breathed his last breath was joyful. Not a chance *that* emotion was invading my soul when I was face-to-face with the realization that I would never experience another second with the love of my life on this side of heaven. Just remembering that painful awareness I felt when looking at Bob's lifeless body brings me chills.

A harsh reality is that suffering can come crashing into your life without warning and without you having any part in its assault. You did nothing to create the crisis, and you certainly weren't expecting it. Illness, accidents, natural disasters, or sudden death can come barreling down on you with the weight and velocity of a freight train. You didn't see it coming, and you can't get out of its way. The crash happens, and you are among the walking wounded. You survived, but its emotional, physical, and mental toll can be devastating. *What just happened?* It is what I call the grief of the unexpected.

In 1986, a tragic story was highlighted in our local Dallas newspaper. A mother and father, Laurie and Ed Bolden, were faced with a heartbreak that reached nightmarish proportions. Their gifted and talented seventeen-year-old son, Allen, a nationally ranked swimmer, worked the summer before entering college as a lifeguard at a local public pool. One night after work, he was kidnapped, robbed, and murdered. For two days, his parents only knew Allen was missing but did not know where he was or if he was alive. His body was found forty-eight hours later. The Boldens were faced with the sudden and harsh reality that their new normal was life without Allen. Oh, the grief of the unexpected!

With a slew of media following his every move, Mr. Bolden said something that has resonated with me to this day. He said, "Pain is mandatory. Suffering is optional."[10] *What?* Pain is mandatory. Suffering is optional. He was acknowledging that pain is part of life.

Your life might not have the immense and cataclysmic horror of such a violent personal loss, but it may be something else that just sucks the very breath out of you. Grief comes in all shapes and sizes and is a natural response to life's painful episodes. Suffering can be endured through lingering and prolonged situations, or it can render you shellshocked through sudden, unexpected disasters or heartbreaks.

The point that Mr. Bolden was making is that *how* you respond to that pain will dictate whether you live victoriously or remain defeated. It is your choice. Many times, you cannot control your circumstances, but you *can* control your responses to your circumstances.

You can choose joy.

"I decided to not let anything else be taken away from me," Laurie Bolden shared with me in the fall of 2019, thirty-four years after the tragedy. "Staying in that grief could have ruined my relationship with my husband and younger son. I looked for where God showed up with His daily mercies. I chose to love God more than anything to keep moving forward."

Life is filled with decisions. Every day, you make dozens of them. Maybe even hundreds.

Some decisions are easy, and some are hard. Some are even downright paralyzing. You can get stuck at the crossroads where faith meets reality. Where belief intersects with doubt. Where confidence collides with mistrust. That is a painful place when your hope is overwhelmed by suffering, suspicion, and skepticism. But the decisions you make and the choices that you embrace will forever impact your attitudes and behavior.

After getting life settled following a crisis, do you decide to choose joy or bitterness and anger? Bitterness is like a cancer, seeking to destroy its host. As the Scripture says, "See to it that no one misses the grace of God and that no bitter root grows up to cause trouble and defile many" (Hebrews 12:15). Bitterness can produce envy, hatred, arrogance, and other attributes that are harmful to those around you. It can destroy relationships. Conversely, joy produces peace, contentment, and confidence that radiate from within, and they are great sources of stability, courage, and healing.

No matter the circumstances surrounding any tragedy, God requests you to make the decision to choose joy even if the grief of the unexpected just flattens you. Given appropriate time and grace to recover, God wants you to move forward in victory with joy even if your heart still really hurts. Your heart can, and probably will, ache for a lifetime.

However, you cannot become a martyr or fall victim to the grief. Hope, faith, and joy will be the balm to soothe and heal the brokenness you feel. Laurie and Ed Bolden are ambassadors of that everlasting truth.

How Do I Do That?

Since God calls you to be joyful, He puts the burden of that mandate on His back by asking you to trust Him. No matter the circumstances or the grief or the chaos—just trust Him!

The prophet Isaiah speaks of peace and serenity for those who trust God. "You will keep in perfect peace him whose mind is steadfast, because he trusts in you" (Isaiah 26:3).

Romans 15:13 speaks further: "May the God of hope fill you with all joy and peace as you trust in Him, so that you may overflow with hope by the power of the Holy Spirit."

The Bible points to God as the giver of hope and hope as the very source of joy. Without hope, joy does not prosper. Without hope, joy cannot thrive within you. It just can't! So to be filled with joy is to have hope. As Romans 15:13 says, trusting in God is what provides a lavish outpouring of hope through the work of the Holy Spirit within you.

Joy is what puts the laughter in your soul and the confidence in your heart. Joy propels you forward. Joy enables you to imagine, create, and believe. It is what causes you to be continually grateful for all that God has done through the life, death, and resurrection of His Son, Jesus Christ. Such joy focuses not on the daily situations involving self but on the tremendous sacrifice of our Savior for you.

God calls you to live joyfully. In God's economy, that is accomplished by trusting Him. Trust is the fuel that ignites you to move forward and smile at the future even when you can't see the end in sight. It is the driver that allows you to be content even when your world is crashing and burning.

Dear friend, be reminded that joy doesn't depend on circumstances, which can be very fleeting. Happiness is an emotion that can be very temporary. One day you are on top of the world, and the next twenty-four hours finds you disappointed, discouraged, or discontented. Emotions can drive you from the mountain peak to the most barren desert overnight … or in just minutes.

Instead, focus on what God has done for you and trust His consistent goodness into the future. That will make you continually thankful and, despite your circumstances, cause you to pause and praise Him. He is your refuge and will never leave you. Self versus Savior. You choose.

Turn Grief into Action

Grief needs a time of quiet recovery. A time to breathe and regather what has been lost. To mend the frayed emotions and to rest the weary soul. Hardships can just wreck your mind, body, and soul, so this healing time needs to be properly applied. If you rebound too quickly, a more painful relapse can be just around the corner. The enemy is salivating to pounce on vulnerable souls. Don't be a casualty to the evil one in your distracted, hurt, and exhausted state.

At the proper time, reaching out to others is a way to begin the healing process. It has been said that grief is not a new emotion, nor is activism a new phenomenon. However, the merging of these two powerful forces begins the road to recovery.

This action of being other-focused rather than self-focused ignites the healing process. Rather than submerging and drowning in the quicksand of pain, you must deal with it head-on. As Mrs. Bolden said after the loss of Allen, "It's like a person losing a leg. I have this gigantic wound that has to heal or I'll die."[11]

The tragedy must be faced. To hide behind closed doors, retreat in isolation, or seek other unhealthy means to deflect it will further the depression and devastation. You must not live in your sorrow. You can't be held hostage to it. You must not carry around a deadened, anaesthetized soul or become an emotional recluse by being immersed in it. You do not want your grief to define you. That will destroy you eventually.

There is a constructive and healthy way to grieve. It is to turn your grief outward, not inward, and reach out to help others. Volunteer for a charity. Get involved in a nonprofit organization that is of interest to you personally and that can use your skills for its betterment.

Champion a cause. Take up a hobby. Being invigorated through the joy of serving others is powerful and can lift you out of the abyss of self-pity, sadness, and hopelessness. Loving selflessly, even during a time of great personal pain, is a sure way to expedite the healing process.

Rise and Shine!

In Psalm 44:23–26, the psalmist shouts out to God in an anguished appeal for help as Israel's army, faithful in its service to the Lord, is being slaughtered and will "face death all day long" by its enemies:

> Awake, O Lord! Why do you sleep?
> Rouse yourself! Do not reject us forever.
> Why do you hide your face and forget our misery and
> oppression?
> We are brought down to the dust; our bodies cling to
> the ground.
> Rise up and help us; redeem us because of your
> unfailing love.

Those seem like pretty powerful accusations against the God of the universe. The psalmist is in deep distress. However, this is a prayer offered to the Lord amid his affliction. He is begging for God's mercy and kindness. He recognizes God reigns with unfailing love and delivers His people even in the direst circumstances. The psalmist acknowledges that even in extreme suffering, the righteous and faithful are not separated from the love of the Lord.

Perhaps we are the ones who need to be awakened. When you are in places of despair, God is not rejecting you or turning His back on you. It is when you are at the end of yourself that your trust in God manifests itself. Have your words of praise been lip service, or do you really mean what Job said during his suffering, "Though he slay me, yet will I hope in him" (Job 13:15)? Can all those hallelujahs ("God be praised!") you so abundantly repeat in the good times be repeated to praise God in the bad? Robert J. Morgan, in his marvelous book *The Red Sea Rules,* offers Rule 2 in moving from fear to faith: "Be more concerned for God's glory than for your relief."[12] You are called to trust and glorify God no matter the circumstances. God is always good, even when your circumstances are not.

When Presbyterian lawyer H. G. Spafford wrote the beloved hymn "It Is Well with My Soul," he penned words fraught with the authentic emotions of one who knew loss well.

On board a ship taking the same route as a vessel that had sunk days earlier in which all four of his daughters drowned (his wife survived), he wrote a moving text in 1873 that continues to inspire us today. (Of note, Mr. Spafford lost a son around the year 1871.)

> When peace like a river, attendeth my way, when
> sorrows and sea billows roll:
>
> Whatever my lot, Thou hast taught me to say, it is
> well, it is well with my soul.

Then the precious refrain that speaks from Mr. Spafford's broken heart:

> It is well with my soul. It is well, it is well with my soul.[13]

Mr. Spafford recognized that whether blessing or darkness governs your life for a season—or longer—your right response is to glorify God and choose joy. It is an intentional choice to bless the name of the Lord and respond with a heart that trusts even when your affliction seems unbearable. That conscious decision will fill your soul with comfort and bring you peace that passes all understanding. You can trust the Creator who spoke the universe into existence. God's power, wisdom, and holiness are unrestricted and infinite. "Ascribe to the Lord the glory due his name; worship the Lord in the splendor of his holiness" (Psalm 29:2). He is worthy of your worship … even when your circumstances are agonizing.

Oh, the grief of the unexpected Mr. Spafford felt! Such sorrow! But he knew he could ultimately choose joy, peace, and calm for his distressed soul. You can too!

Joy Killers

The enemy of your soul has many weapons he successfully uses to steal your joy. Remember his job description from John 10:10: "The thief comes only to steal and kill and destroy." Stealing your joy is a full assault tactic. And he uses many subtle and not-so-subtle tactics to accomplish his mission.

The enemy uses *comparison* to steal your joy. You look at other people and think they are so much smarter, prettier, and more sophisticated than you are. They have so many more talents than your pitiful few, if any. You have so little to offer because their contributions are bigger, greater, and more important.

Comparison is so treacherous and meaningless in the eyes of God, who made each one of us so uniquely special and different. No one is like you. All of us have different callings, gifts, and purposes. You are not meant to be like anyone else. Quite frankly, other people's qualities have nothing to do with the glorious assets God designed specifically for you. The ways you are wired, look, and act are unique to you and no one else. Your lifetime should be spent taking the allotment of abilities God has purposefully given you and doing the most with them. Period. That is what He wants. You waste your time and emotional energy when you compare yourself to others. Our perfect Creator knew what He was doing when He created wonderful and unique *you*! As Irish poet and playwright Oscar Wilde wrote, "Be yourself; everyone else is already taken."[14] Celebrate your uniqueness!

The enemy uses *bad experiences* to steal your joy. Your parents were abusive. An unwise decision was damaging. Destruction, death, and disease manufactured grief beyond consolation. But God says you are worthy of His love no matter the circumstances. An unloving earthly father has no claim on the fatherhood of God, who loves so deeply, unconditionally, and completely. A poor decision is forgiven by the One who offered His Son for the forgiveness of all sins.

Life's calamities and heartaches are cradled in the hands of the One who says, "Come to me, all you who are weary and burdened, and I will give you rest" (Matthew 11:28). Who says, "I will never leave you nor forsake you" (Joshua 1:5). Of whom Scripture speaks, "He is my loving God and my fortress, my stronghold and my deliverer, my shield, in whom I take refuge" (Psalm144:2). Indeed, you are instructed to "cast all your anxiety on him because he cares for you" (1 Peter 5:7). No matter if your past has been harmed by your own decisions or by circumstances beyond your control, God is the "refuge for the oppressed, a stronghold in times of trouble" (Psalm 9:9). So wrap your joy in the forgiveness, power, and protection of God's love.

The enemy uses *fear* to steal your joy. Oh, the power of fear! God did give you fear to keep you safe when circumstances, relationships, or decisions can potentially be hurtful, damaging, or even dangerous. A healthy dose of reasonable fear, when used correctly, keeps you out of trouble and free from harm. That's all good. But fear is also a mighty weapon of the evil one. It can be crippling. Fear paralyzes you to move forward with mighty plans. Fear destroys your confidence and limits your thoughts, emotions, and efforts. Fear relentlessly stalks and intimidates you. Your best performance can never be achieved when fear grips your heart and unsteadies your hands.

God doesn't want you in miserable bondage to fear. Scripture states very clearly, "For God did not give us a spirit of timidity, but a spirit of power, of love and of self-discipline" (2 Timothy 1:7). He is your strength when you confidently trust Him. Your trust unleashes His unlimited power through which flows hope, courage, and peace to a distressed soul. Whether you are amid chaos or licking your wounds from a recent mistake, God is there. Do not let the evil one's stranglehold of fear grasp you. Psalm 27:1 says, "The LORD is my light and my salvation—whom shall I fear? The LORD is the stronghold of my life—of whom shall I be afraid?" The resounding answer is *no one*! God's perfect love casts out fear and provides the freedom and peace you need to move forward. As Jesus proclaims in John 14:27, "Peace I leave with you; my peace I give you. I do not give to you as the world gives. Do not let your hearts be troubled and do not be afraid." Be at peace, my friend!

Worry doesn't get you there either. Worrying is simply taking responsibility God never intended you to have. Give all your challenges to God. He can handle them! Worry is an effective tool used by the enemy to confuse, distract, and weaken your resolve. Agonizing over the what-ifs, fretting over past or future decisions, or stewing over inadequate resources for the journey ahead are fruitless wastes of time and energy. That creates heavy burdens to carry, which God never intended you to do.

The Scriptures warn against worry:

Who of you by worrying can add a single hour to his
life? Since you cannot do this very little thing, why do
you worry about the rest? (Luke 12:25–26)

Don't let the enemy use worry to thwart your daily communion with God and to disrupt the joy that results from that close relationship.

The enemy also uses *discouragement* to steal our joy. Famed football coach Vince Lombardi once said, "It's not whether you get knocked down; it's whether you get up."[15] It's impossible to do anything productive when you are down for the count. Once you are back on your feet, you can put those sneakers to work! And Coach Lombardi knew that tackles don't just happen on a football field. They happen in living rooms. Schoolrooms. Boardrooms. It's extremely hard to be joyful when your heart is heavy with a sense of frustration, disappointment, or lack of confidence. Your defenses are depleted and can easily succumb to the opinions, judgment, and criticism of others, including yourself.

Sometimes your own voice is the harshest and most accusatory. Discouragement depletes any hopefulness for a positive outcome and only focuses on the endless possibilities of failure.

Scripture calls the devil the father of lies. He will do anything to strip you of dignity, honor, and self-assurance. He knows how to silence your courage, erode your confidence, and weaken your convictions. Deuteronomy 31:6, 8 is a strong battle cry against the attack of discouragement. It is Moses's command to all of Israel, at the end of their forty-year wilderness wandering, to cross the Jordan and take possession of the land that God had promised to their forefathers generations ago. Moses said, "Be strong and courageous. Do not be afraid or terrified…. The LORD himself goes before you and will be with you; he will never leave you nor forsake you. Do not be afraid; do not be discouraged."

God is the general on this bloodied battlefield that can leave you shredded and shattered. The enemy has no authority over God. Do not listen to his accusatory voice. Instead, God promises He will never forsake you. He goes with you. Be encouraged! You have a mighty Warrior battling for your victory!

Habakkuk's Hang-Up

It has been over twenty-six hundred years since the prophet Habakkuk lived during a corrupt, oppressive, and spiritually dark time in Judah. Habakkuk had at first pleaded with God to intervene and punish the perversity and injustice prevalent in Judah. But God didn't answer the prophet's prayers. Instead, in 605 BC, He gave Habakkuk a vision of an impending invasion by the cruel and violent Babylonians against Jerusalem (Judah's capital) in 597 BC that would result in Jerusalem being pillaged and its people being deported to Babylon. Habakkuk was struggling to understand how God would allow such a thing to happen. Habakkuk's agitated dialogues with God were full of angry complaints that God would accept the unlawful Babylonians, characterized as "ruthless and impetuous people," as the victors in this conquest. Though Judah had drifted from integrity and righteousness as a nation, this vision of Judah's impending doom from an even more wicked and arrogant nation had Habakkuk bewildered and firing complaints at God. He says, "Your eyes are too pure to look on evil; you cannot tolerate wrong. Why then do you tolerate the treacherous? Why are you silent while the wicked swallow up those more righteous than themselves?" (Habakkuk 1:13).

You can feel Habakkuk losing patience with God. He just seems to be screaming with furious accusations: "How can a holy God allow this injustice to happen? *What are You doing?*" Do those words sound familiar in your own voice? Have you ever faulted God with similar accusations?

In his angry state, Habakkuk waited for God's response. He was wise to stop and direct his attention to God in hopeful anticipation of what He would do. Habakkuk trusted God. Instead of continuing to try to figure things out in his confused mindset, he waited on God to reveal His plans.

God did not disappoint Habakkuk. He spoke. He told of the future fall and annihilation of Babylon that would happen approximately sixty-six years after Habakkuk's vision. God graphically pronounced five woes against Babylon's idolatrous, unjust, and greedy disgrace. As He condemned Babylon with His harsh accusations, God contrasted that with the encouragement that "the righteous will live by his faith" (Habakkuk 2:4). Here God reveals that His people must wait patiently on Him and that faith is an intentional act of trusting in His sovereignty.

One of my favorite passages in Scripture is Habakkuk 3:17–19. This final prayer is Habakkuk's joyful profession of faith and thankfulness in God regardless of any circumstances. He has learned to patiently wait and trust his Savior-God even during hardships, suffering, or uncertainty.

> Though the fig tree does not bud and there are no grapes on the vines, though the olive crop fails and the fields produce no food, though there are no sheep in the pen and no cattle in the stalls, yet I will rejoice in the LORD, I will be joyful in God my Savior.
>
> The Sovereign LORD is my strength; he makes my feet like the feet of a deer, he enables me to go on the heights.

Habakkuk's words of trust, joy, and adoration proclaiming his Savior-God are recognized as one of the strongest affirmations of faith in all Scripture. He recognized that circumstances were not grounds to alter his relationship with God. Habakkuk acknowledged that trusting in the Lord always and giving thanks to Him, no matter what he was facing or knew was ahead, were the surest ways to experience hope.

In the same way, God has designed you to worship Him through trusting His goodness … even if that requires waiting. Living in deep dependence on God allows you to glorify God in any circumstance. You have cheerful confidence in knowing He will deliver. The enemy cannot quiet the hearts of obedient and faithful people—even in the face of the most extreme or difficult circumstances. You can choose joy!

Chapter Summary Points

- Wounds do not heal overnight; allow time to grieve.
- God calls you to be joyful despite the grief of the unexpected and any new normal.
- Many times, you cannot control your circumstances, but you can control your responses to your circumstances. You can choose joy!
- Joy is an intentional choice not based on your circumstances but on your relationship with God.
- Focus on what God has done for you and trust His consistent goodness. It may involve waiting.
- God is glorious even when your circumstances are not.
- Pain is mandatory but suffering is optional, depending on how you respond.
- Deal with your loss rather than immersing yourself in it or becoming a victim to it.
- Healing begins by focusing on others rather than on yourself.
- The enemy uses the joy killers of comparison, bad experiences, fear, worry, and discouragement to generate hopelessness.

Takeaway Question

How can you find joy in your suffering?

Applications: Eight Ways to Choose Joy

- Turn your grief into action.
  - Volunteer at your favorite charity or nonprofit organization.
  - Find activities that focus on others rather than on yourself to avoid depression, pity, or isolation
  - Take up a new hobby that brings you personal satisfaction and excitement.

- Share your feelings with people who have had similar experiences or who are compassionate listeners.
  - Join a support group that focuses on the same issues that have broken your heart and that leave you hopeless or grieving.
  - Create opportunities for social interaction with others rather than inwardly suffering in silence or without support.
  - Surround yourself with positive, productive, and joyful people who will add optimism and hope to your life.

- Savor the memories of good health, time with loved ones, and joyful experiences that have defined your life rather than consistently focusing on what has been lost.

- Allow yourself to grieve for a time or season but then recognize that God wants to use this situation for good, and think of ways it can be turned into a platform to help others or champion a cause.

- Assess the ways that your hardship or suffering has brought about good changes in your life.

- Identify your joy killers.
  - Recognize what triggers such feelings.
  - Discuss these events and feelings with a trusted friend or support group to walk you through them.
  - Confess these joy killers to the Lord and immediately call out the enemy when they are creeping back so that the devil does not get a foothold.

- Thank God for the provisions He has given through hard times and for the ways He has consistently lavished you with favor and abundance.

- Stay rooted in God's Word, promises, and plans so that hope flourishes and joy results.

The joy of the LORD is your strength.

(Nehemiah 8:10)

CHAPTER 4

RESTORING COMMUNITY

You Need Community

Going alone never works. It does not go well with anyone who thinks, *I don't need help to lift this!* We might think we are capable enough, strong enough, or even brave enough to tackle something solo, but the reality is that being undergirded with the faithfulness, commitment, and dedication of others provides a safe and comforting refuge during personal turmoil and hardship. It is called community.

A community of friends prays with you through your tough times, uses their backs to carry you, and extends their hands to reach out and hold you up. A community of friends genuinely cheers with you from the mountaintops and weeps with you in the desert. A community of friends holds you accountable for your actions, rebukes you when you make imprudent decisions, and guides you back to restoration. These important people have your best interests at heart, and any constructive counsel is done out of love and for your personal benefit rather than with abusive intentions or negative condemnation.

Regularly engaging in a healthy core community of encouragers breathes life back into suffocating souls. It helps you make wiser decisions and participate in actions that will be much more beneficial to you and others. Given all that the enemy throws your way to discourage, discredit, and delay you in moving forward with confidence and joy, you need friends who will be able to assess the situation calmly and wisely and offer you sound counsel.

What Does God Say to Do?

Ecclesiastes 4:9–12 speaks to the importance of this issue:

> Two are better than one, because they have a good
> return for their work:
> If one falls down, his friend can help him up.
> But pity the man who falls and has no one to help
> him up!
> Also, if two lie down together, they will keep warm.
> But how can one keep warm alone?
> Though one may be overpowered, two can defend
> themselves.
> A cord of three strands is not quickly broken.

Community was God's idea to begin with. His Word clearly shows us we need one another. It does not go well for someone to live in isolation or without the protection, support, and advocacy of another. This idea of *community* reflects God's desire that you be in unity and harmony with others. You are part of something bigger than yourself for your well-being internally and externally.

Community is a support system that gives *in abundance* when you are depleted, loves without condemnation, and acts as a shield when life's fiery ordeals are aimed at you with full fury. It is the use of another advocate for your protection. That person shows up when you are going down. God purposefully set those relationships in motion through the value of community.

What Else Does God Say?

God is not done talking about this! Genesis 2:18 says, "The LORD God said, 'It is not good for the man to be alone. I will make a helper suitable for him.'" God understood that His newly created man, Adam, needed a companion, so He created Eve as his partner. Someone to do life with. God knew humanity would not do well alone and isolated.

Even though Adam and Eve gave in to temptation and were expelled from the glorious environment God had prepared for them to fully enjoy, propelling them and all future generations into a state of fallen humanity, they needed each other to bear life's burdens, sorrows, and joys. Similarly, you and I need people in our lives because we have a way of making big messes of things. It just comes so naturally! It has a name—sin. And the outcome can be brutal. Whether they are family or friends, God knew we needed the inner sanctum of community rather than go it alone to help thrive in a world where hope and joy are forever challenged by strife and struggle.

As the early church was being formed, the fellowship among those new believers was done in a spirit of unity, joy, and oneness. Acts 2:46 outlined these activities: They broke bread in their homes and ate together with glad and sincere hearts, praising God and enjoying the favor of all the people. Additionally, they also devoted themselves to worshipping together in the temple. The idea of fellowship in God's economy is surrounding yourself with people who are steadfast in their support of you, praying for you, and being a devoted friend.

Relationships Are Blessings from God

C. S. Lewis's book *The Four Loves* speaks to the power of friendship as a God-ordained blessing. The Almighty sets this priority in motion.

In friendship, we think we have chosen our peers.
In reality, a few years' difference in the dates of our
births, a few more miles between certain houses,
the choice of one university instead of another, the
accident of a topic being raised or not raised at a
first meeting—any of these chances might have
kept us apart. But, for a Christian, there are, strictly
speaking, no chances. A secret Master of Ceremonies
has been at work. Christ, who said to the disciples,
"you have not chosen me, but I have chosen you,"
can truly say to every group of Christian friends, "you
have not chosen one another but I have chosen you
for one another." The friendship is not a reward for
our discrimination and good taste in finding one
another out. It is the instrument by which God reveals
to each of us the beauties of all the others.[16]

What a glorious way to look at community. Relationships are a gift from God. Since the beginning of time, God knew the value of strong friendships and enduring relationships to undergird you in times of need and to celebrate with you in times of rejoicing. People who are an extra set of eyes and ears and who will fight for your welfare make life easier to navigate when those storms hit. Whether for protection, provision, encouragement, or counsel, a strong bond of friends will bring joy and security throughout the challenges of daily living.

How important it is to surround yourself with wise, kind, and supportive friends who have your back. There will always be people who want to bring you down through their jealousy, abusiveness, and greed. Sadly, people's insecurities fuel their deep desires to reduce your success and increase theirs. Having a small inner sanctum of authentic friends will help diffuse destructive behaviors from those people.

God knows you need people who help you work through the weak areas in your life that keep resurfacing and creating havoc. People who are honest with you but who breathe life into you no matter how badly you've made a mess of things are the people you want in your inner circle. They feed your soul even when they are instructing you on how to be more mature, wise, and healthy in your behavior.

We All Need to Belong Somewhere!

Going alone on life's journey never works. Hopelessness wraps itself in isolation and loneliness. No one to listen. Nowhere to go. No way to move forward. The dark place seems like an abyss. The enemy likes to pronounce words of destruction, insults, and slander when you have no loyal comrade to challenge those lies and deceptions. You begin to believe that you are unqualified, unsuited, and unstable to pursue your dreams, make things happen, or have meaningful relationships. That voice spews toxic insults simply to implode your confidence and undermine your goals. The enemy is most effective and successful in this cruel treachery when you are alone with only your reduced and broken sense of self. The enemy delights in besieging those who have no steadfast buddies to challenge his lies.

Without the objective wisdom and encouragement of others who truly care about you, it is easy to believe flawed opinions about yourself strengthened by insults from abusive relationships and wounded individuals whose own insecurities propel them to degrade others. It is also easy to fall prey to unhealthy habits or destructive behaviors that serve to anesthetize your lonely soul.

COVID-19 exposed the perils of isolation and distance from community. Multiple studies were undertaken regarding the pandemic's toll on increased alcohol usage, depression, and anxiety. The impact of binge and heavy drinking, as reported by Healthline.com, stated the following:

- Unhealthy binge drinking increased 14% overall and 17% among women (measured on days per month that alcohol was consumed), with average consumption increasing one day more per month by three of four adults.
- Additionally, researchers said heavy drinking rose 41% among women and that one of every five women surveyed had heavily consumed alcohol at least one additional day per month as compared with the previous year.
- COVID restrictions and closed meetings prevented people from attending counseling and twelve-step programs to get the support they needed, making recovery from alcohol use disorder difficult and contributing to isolation and fueling the inability to cope with the lack of support that had previously been received.[17]

The Centers for Disease Control and Prevention reported on the increased mental stress toll of COVID-19:

- 11% of US adults reported symptoms of anxiety and depression from January through June 2019.[18]
- 33.9% of US adults reported symptoms of anxiety and depression by May 14-19, 2020.[19]
- 42% of US adults reported symptoms of anxiety and depression in December 2020.[20]

On May 2, 2023, US Surgeon General Dr. Vivek Murthy announced that loneliness and isolation posed a public health threat. He said loneliness created health risks as deadly as smoking up to fifteen cigarettes a day. In an eighty-one-page report from his office, the surgeon general said about half of US adults admit they have experienced loneliness, which has mental and physical health consequences like great risk of anxiety, depression, dementia, heart disease, and stroke. He declared loneliness as a public health epidemic that deeply worsened with COVID-19's negative impact of isolation from family members, workplaces, schools, community groups, and houses of worship.

The psychological impact of isolation, fear, and stress can deteriorate coping mechanisms. Frustrations and edginess can produce a sense of hopelessness and darkness.

However, hope is ushered in through a community of close people surrounding you with support, prayers, and encouragement. Social connections are essential for your emotional welfare, strength, and health. Being in a community of people who reassure you in the bad times, gently rebuke you in the wayward times, and wisely counsel you in the uncertain times is a safe place to park your humanness. You are not alone! No assault from those who seek to harm you can create lasting collateral damage when your heart and soul are protected by the heavy defense artillery of a loving community group. We all need to belong *somewhere*!

The Necessity and Beauty of Community

When Bob was sick, love walked through our front door regularly in all heights, ages, and nationalities. Some had gray hair. Some spoke with foreign accents. Some were just learning their multiplication tables.

While we fought for Bob's life, a community of people rallied behind us. They brought food. They prayed over Bob and anointed his head with oil. They organized prayer services for him. They wrote notes of great encouragement. (Bob received more than five thousand cards and letters!)

Since so many of Bob's and my friends wanted to visit him but his weak immune-suppressed condition would not allow these dear people to join us at the hospital or at our home during much of his illness, one gifted and kind artist friend, Kate Juett, hand-painted multiple exquisite posters that we taped to our hospital room door and to our front door at home for those who wanted to come by and write a note of encouragement for Bob. How that lifted his spirits! How that allowed our friends to have the satisfaction of being able to share their heartfelt sentiments so Bob would know they were praying for and thinking about him. What a sweet gift Kate provided us!

Stephen Nielson, a world-famous concert pianist and wonderful friend, came to our home when he was not touring to give Bob glorious private recitals on our woefully untuned piano. (Candidly, tuning the piano was a low priority during our cancer journey!) Bob lay in bed down the hall, too weak to venture outside our bedroom, but he insisted his pain subsided during those splendid private concerts.

My treasured friend Connie Yates consistently left Big Red soda on our front porch when Bob suffered through chemo treatments. "It's the only thing my sister could drink to combat her nausea when going through chemo for her breast cancer. I hope it helps Bob too!" Connie would tell me.

One night, Bob's blood transfusion ran long and finished up well past midnight. I had left the hospital earlier to put William to bed. Now, Bob was ready to come home. What to do? I looked out my window and saw our dear neighbor's light on across the street. I called. Mary Miller answered as cheerfully as she would have at two o'clock in the afternoon. I said, "Mary, what are you doing up at this hour? It's after midnight!"

"Waiting for your call," she replied. She came over and spent half the night at our home while I picked up my exhausted husband.

Bob needed some strong pain medicine on a Sunday afternoon. Since I couldn't leave Bob, Bill Moore, our fabulous next-door neighbor, offered to help. Within minutes of Bill leaving to fetch the medicine, the sky opened, and every ounce of water poured from the heavenlies! Dallas witnessed a monsoon that Sunday! Bill faced some issues picking up the medicine. *Five hours later,* he returned with the medicine, a soaked man having just sacrificed his entire Sunday afternoon for us. His response? He asked to do more next time!

Bob and I knew we had warriors fighting for us on a bloodied battlefield where death was on the offense and gaining ground. Many nights, Bob woke up at two thirty in the morning and said, "I am in such pain, but I know *right now* someone is praying for me. What great comfort!"

The stories of selflessness were endless. The hands and feet of kind, thoughtful, and generous people were moving, running, and reaching out to the Simmons family—a family who was exhausted and in need. Perhaps *in crisis* was the better word. Certainly, our life felt stuck on hold, but we were surrounded by an army of people who prayed for us, cared for us, and sacrificed for us. It buoyed Bob's spirit and fed his soul even when his body was declining. That is the beauty of community.

What Does Community Look Like?

Where do you find this community of people? It should be a small group of cherished friends (or those whom you feel confident will develop into close friends) whom you know can be trusted with your feelings. These people will know everything about you in due time, so they have to be individuals you can share life with—and that means with its good, bad, and ugly! They are your go-to people. We are talking a small group of people. You might already be able to identify a few. Some might be found within your place of worship. Some might be business colleagues, volunteer comrades, or former high school or college buddies. The idea is to develop a few close friends who will walk with you through the dark places in life as well as celebrate with you from the mountaintops.

Perhaps you can corral these three to six people to join you in a group setting once a week, twice a month, or once a month. At that time, you can collectively share your experiences and positively encourage and/or counsel each other on next steps to resolve or celebrate life's opportunities staring you, and them, in the face.

My community group has met weekly in my home since January 2012. We call ourselves the Seeker Sisters. We are currently a posse of four—Jo Tiller, Lynn McDonough, Vicki Hitzges, and me. We are a diverse group that has morphed over the years. Our other community group members have moved, changed churches, gone into grief recovery, or just taken a break. We come from different backgrounds, ethnicities, and life experiences. We share opposing political views. We have dissimilar ways of coping with big life issues. We are not homogenous but, rather, uniquely varied in the way we view the world, its people, and its flaws.

However, that spectrum of difference is what makes our community group so rich in depth, profound in counsel, and broad in perspective. The glue that binds the diverse ways we are wired is our love for the Lord. That common shared faith unites us and draws us so close. We do Bible studies, talk real-life struggles, and share prayer requests. We text one another almost daily with words of encouragement and scriptural references. There are times we never get to discuss our Bible lesson for the evening because some personal issues are just too heavy and need the full two hours of discussion.

Lots has gone down with my Seeker Sisters over these many years. Some good things. Some challenging things. Some really devastating things. The Kleenex box gets emptied at many of our weekly gatherings. But any wounded hearts that walk through my front door leave encouraged every week because we are committed to one another's emotional, spiritual, physical, and mental health. The compassion of community—its sheer force tackles hopelessness.

I have also been blessed with a group of four devoted friends whom I have known for over thirty-five years—Mary Dowling, Betty Lovell, Jackie Thornton, and Connie Yates. We call ourselves the Fave Five. During decades of our life journey together, our seasons of womanhood have all been different. One has never married. One is married with no children. One was married with grandchildren (she subsequently lost her wonderful husband a decade ago.) One is divorced. I am widowed. Our age difference spans twenty-one years. The Fave Five is fervently committed to one another. We get together regularly throughout the year with dinners and shared events, email or text one another multiple times weekly, and have at least one annual reunion over a weekend. We have supported one another through surgeries, loss of loved ones, crises, joys, sorrows, and everything in between. We challenge one another. We encourage one another. We have one another's backs. And we have desperately needed one another in the span of well over three decades.

Meg Adams has been my prayer partner for thirty years. Suzanne Schutze has been a very close personal friend for over forty years. Dianne Ogle has advised me, prayed for me, and been my encourager, my Barnabas (and that is what I call her), for thirty years. The list goes on …

In my seasons of joy and sorrow, I couldn't imagine life without these fabulous friends who form my community. They have protected my soul, guarded my heart, and loved me unconditionally. Oh, the value of community!

Community in Action: Stretcher Bearers

In her very honest, soul-bearing, and heartrending book *When I Lay My Isaac Down*, popular author and distinguished speaker Carol Kent shares the unimaginable journey she and her husband Gene have taken since October 24, 1999. On that fateful day, their twenty-five-year-old son Jason Paul

(JP), a graduate of the US Naval Academy with a distinguished military record, shot and killed his wife's ex-husband outside a busy restaurant in Orlando. JP was given a sentence of life in prison without parole despite several appeals.

For the Kents, this heavy sorrow left their emotions raw and depleted. But hope stepped in through the caring actions of men and women who bore the burdens of this needy and grieving couple. She called these helping saints her Stretcher Bearers. They were people of encouragement who lifted and carried the Kents through their brokenness and darkness. They emailed. They sent cards and gifts. They prayed. They wept with and for the Kents. They stood strong when the Kents were exhausted. Carol wrote the job description of her unshakable Stretcher Bearers:

> Until I found myself flat-out needy, I never understood what the power of community could do. It's people in the body of Christ working like a family to sit and cry with you. Holding you. Caring for your needs. Carrying your burden for a day. Creatively solving problems. Gathering resources. Opening doors of hope. Writing notes of encouragement. Fighting a cause on your behalf. Finding a way when there is no way. Listening. Waiting with you as long as it takes. It's people being "Jesus" to you.[21]

Carol dedicates her book to the Stretcher Bearers and "to all of you who take the time to respond to the needs of others by answering the question, 'How can I help with tangible encouragement?'"

Apostle Paul writes to the early church, "Carry each other's burdens, and in this way you will fulfill the law of Christ" (Galatians 6:2). A paralyzed person cannot move. A person on life support cannot skip and jump. An exhausted person cannot function well. Carol and Gene Kent felt that they were emotionally, physically, and mentally crippled. They needed to be carried to have any hope of forward movement. Their Stretcher Bearers, showing the love and goodness of Christ, allowed them to see small streaks of daylight from their dark hole of brokenness.

"The Lord is close to the brokenhearted," proclaims Psalm 34:18. This verse is a heartfelt tribute to God's design to comfort those who are broken to the core. His plan is to use Stretcher Bearers and community groups to distribute His tender mercies, abundant grace, and limitless loving-kindness. Such compassionate hands and feet can press forward to move the immovable, mend the broken, and inspire the hopeless. It's the power in multiples when one is the loneliest number.

Letting Go of Pride

My dad lived large. He loved fast motorcycles and fast horses. While very deliberate and methodical with his wisdom, talents, and integrity in the professional arena, Dad only knew to operate at laser speed on the athletic field. He was a well-trained athlete, having been selected as an alternate on the 1952 Olympics team (equestrian) and having competed in the 1954 Modern Pentathlon. Dad ultimately parlayed his devotion for riding into playing polo. I marveled at how he could stay on that horse going up and down the field at breakneck speeds. Yes, he did have multiple trips to the hospital with broken ribs, collarbones, and fingers, but he could never wait to get back on that polo pony. Then in January 1993, his horse was T-boned by another during a polo match. Dad and horse were pummeled to the ground. He went immediately into a coma with a severe head injury.

When my friends heard of the accident, help came a callin'! However, I resisted at first. I was always the one who had been the giver. I had always been the first responder to bring food, write a note, or encourage a person.

With my dad's crisis, I was not so receptive to being the one in need. I was strong enough to help handle Dad's injury. I didn't require others to pitch in. Initially, my pride did not allow me to receive the glorious benefits of love, care, and concern from others that I so desperately needed.

It takes humility to be the recipient of another's kindness. When your mental and emotional resources are drained, you have to rely on others so you don't experience personal bankruptcy—the kind that has nothing to do with money. It is a loss that grips the very fiber of your feelings and the core of your emotions. It is humbling to accept help from others. It is hard to tell your friends you are hurting or you have done something unwise or you have a hidden sin that needs to be addressed. It can be uncomfortable to say you don't have it all together. That your heart is breaking. That you don't know how to take the next step forward. However, you desperately need to share your limitations with those you trust before you implode from within! Do not let pride keep you from receiving the great gift of encouragement and help from people wanting to serve.

I was so grateful that the Secchis, our beloved neighbors across the street at the time, invited Bob over for dinners on a regular basis when I was out of town visiting Dad in rehab where the accident occurred. Their incredible hospitality sustained Bob many evenings and lightened his load as he dealt with this crushing incident.

I am grateful for the outstretched arms of those who sought to relieve my pain. Without even knowing it, learning to be the humble and thankful recipient of other people's sweet compassion during Dad's accident and recovery prepared me for Bob's unexpected cancer diagnosis nine years later.

Victims versus Victors

Some people live in the past ... as victims. They let the memory of being relationally "cheated" implode their lives. Whether consciously or unconsciously, they play the victim card. It's everyone else's fault. Bad parents. Bad spouses. Bad friends. Bad teachers. Bad breaks. My head is spinning with the excuses and reasons victims give for relinquishing any responsibility in moving forward.

But I get it. There are some frightfully abusive parents in the world. There are some very sad circumstances of good fathers or mothers dying young (I know firsthand) or of cheating spouses or of jealous coworkers or of unfair employers. There are accidents or health issues that suddenly change lives without warning. There are betrayals and hurts in every shape and size. Life can be really tough—and unjust—and painful. So many people just stay in that role of victim because they either have no hand reaching out to pull them from that abyss, or they choose to remain there indefinitely. Either way, they are alone.

Living in chaos is easier at times than summoning up the courage to move forward. However, in isolation, you allow the person inflicting the pain to have the power. You give authority to the enemy, who tells you over and over again that you are not worthy to be loved or to be successful or to experience true joy. But a community of encouragers will strip the control from the devious messenger(s) and remind you that God has full authority over all. Walk as a victor in the middle of a setback because the enemy is under the sovereign hand of God. The Lord is in charge; the enemy is not. Nor are those painful memories or failed experiences of the past that the enemy delights in bringing up to prevent you from living in victory. Do not give them power.

Live in the present rather than drifting back to past disappointments or mistakes that hold you hostage in that victim role.

God's sweet restoration of fulfillment and joy in your brokenness is made possible through the relationships of people who care. God desires you to be in unity and harmony with others. This community of advocates quickly responds when one of their own falls prey to the world's lies. Loyalty and love are too powerful for the enemy's assaults because they provide other robust and stout warriors, prepared to do battle, to rescue their wounded comrade. When that committed and plentiful band of warriors is fighting on your behalf, encouraging you with words of affirmation and truth, the enemy is doomed. He has no power over you. The victory is yours!

The Power of Mentorship

"As iron sharpens iron, so one person sharpens another" (Proverbs 27:17). OK. You've heard that. Iron sharpens iron. What are the practical applications? Literally, there is mutual benefit as two blades are rubbed against each other to sharpen the edges for effective use. Likewise, you are meant to be in constant fellowship to sharpen another through interaction in all seasons of life. The additional power of mentorship allows experienced people to help you live intentionally, increase your talents, and learn from failure. A mentor coaches you to make wise decisions to be a productive, respected, and honorable leader both personally and professionally.

Mentors are people who deliver invaluable words of encouragement, discernment, and instruction, with the purpose to teach and train. While your parents have an enormous impact on your development, whether positive or negative, mentors are usually people outside your family whose successful experiences influence healthy lifestyle habits, character growth, and professional expertise. It is also easier for those outside the periphery of parenthood to patiently instruct a younger generation.

When my mother gave me my first tennis lesson at age eight, disaster struck. Mom recounted the moment in one of her monthly columns she penned for *Tennis* magazine. She wrote:

Anyone who has worked with his child on school studies knows the innate frustrations. ... This situation, sad to relate, carries over into other fields, as illustrated to me when I took my daughter Cynthia to the local tennis center. ... If I lost my child's confidence on the tennis court, what chance had I at modern math?!? ... The first few shots went beautifully. But then I choked! I mis-hit a forehand and the ball landed a good racquet length away from Cindy. With a disdainful look, she inquired why I couldn't hit the ball *closer* to her. *"After all, mommy, you've been playing tennis long enough."* A few bumbling, apologetic words were uttered and on we went. Midway through the lesson I noticed Cindy favoring a Western grip on the forehand. ... I suggested an Eastern grip and adjusted her hand accordingly. The inevitable happened—she couldn't hit a ball over the net. *"Think I'll go back to my way,"* she said. *"It works much better."* And so it went through the hour. Cindy even sensed my utter dejection for as we walked off court a little arm slipped around my waist.

"Maybe you'll do better next time, mommy," said Cindy ... *hopefully.*[22]

What nerve! What eight-year-old feistiness! I still cringe knowing that thousands of people reading Mom's column in the 1960s were exposed to Little Mo's sassy daughter! But this situation magnifies how difficult it is for a parent to teach a child anything—particularly a skill at a younger age. Let me be crystal clear. Parents *must* teach their children values and virtues that will help them master the skill of living. That is their responsibility. Children need to be raised with guardians who exemplify standards and ethics that promote integrity, kindness, courage, faithfulness, gratitude, humility, and compassion. That critical instruction cannot be left up to schools, churches, or other institutions to do in place of parents. However, there is an important space to be occupied by mentors to help guide and nurture those under their valued instruction.

When I lost my beloved Bob, I had nine-year-old William, who was only the second boy on my mother's side in five generations. I realized I needed some help on certain male-oriented issues then and as William grew older. I am grateful for the coaches, dads, teachers, and friends I selected to walk William through some testosterone-laden pathways I had no clue how to traverse.

My wonderful dad was very instrumental in navigating William through treacherous paths and modeling how to be an ethical, effective, and strong leader. I was fortunate to have some supportive fathers of William's friends ask William and me to participate in an excellent father-son curriculum for nine months. I read lots of books on how to raise boys, but William needed men, not a mom trying to act like a dad, to help explain things in which I would have looked like a deer in headlights. I was engaged every bit of the way but recognized William's need to have men speak into his life. Many of those men are still very much a part of his life today.

I had a brilliant mentor in business, Stan Levenson, who later became my business partner when we merged our public relations firms. Stan is considered a distinguished master in the public relations, media communications, and integrated marketing industry as well as one of the finest and most respected gentlemen in the business. I grew in my craft just by emulating his enormous talents and having him share his decades of experience with me. Now retired, he and his wife, Barbara, remain two of my dearest friends.

Mentors have such an important role in offering support and a lifeline to valuable feedback and encouragement. They are part of an arsenal of community leaders who sharpen you and present solutions to problems.

They provide sound advice based on their breadth of experience. The bond that exists in a mentor-mentee relationship rewards and transforms.

Note to Self

My friend, a word of caution: be careful whom you follow. There are people who suggest they are God. Or that they have supernatural powers. Or that they can provide a future that will lavish you with abundance. Beware! These people look just like you and me. They want your money. They want your allegiance. They want your contacts. As William would say, "They are posers!" Fake, phony, and fraudulent. They will scam you and run. Be careful. They can be dangerous and lure the unsuspecting into their deceitful and diabolical perversion. There is only one true God. There is only one Creator of heaven and earth. The Scriptures reveal His holiness, perfection, and glory.

> Not to us, O LORD, not to us but to your name be the
> glory, because of your love and faithfulness.
> (Psalm 115:1)

> Holy, holy, holy is the LORD Almighty; the whole earth
> is full of his glory. (Isaiah 6:3)

> "I am the Alpha and the Omega," says the Lord
> God, "who is, and who was, and who is to come, the
> Almighty." (Revelation 1:8)

Guard yourself against posers. There are business, ministry, and cultural leaders who deserve your admiration and pursuit. There are good coaches and mentors in their areas of expertise. As you evaluate leaders to consider as role models, ask the question, Are they worthy to be followed? You and

I can name some fine individuals who are marked by excellence and who have distinguished themselves as remarkable servant-leaders. Allow their resilience, compassion, and skillful example to be magnified in your life. However, at the same time, recognize there is only One who is worthy of our worship and adoration. He is the Lord God Almighty!

Chapter Summary Points

- Life is relational.
- Relationships are a gift from God.
- Social connections are essential for your encouragement, strength, and protection.
- Everyone needs to belong somewhere—it is called community.
- Community is a small group of trusted, compassionate, and engaged people committed to the mental, emotional, physical, and spiritual health of its members.
- Hope is ushered in through the support, dedication, and compassion of community.
- Those in crisis depend on the outstretched hands of others to be able to move forward.
- Being alone and isolated can generate hopelessness and despair as the enemy besieges those who have no loyal comrades to challenge his lies and deceit.
- Allowing people to meet your needs and carry your burdens requires surrendering pride.
- Have victory over your setbacks rather than be victimized by them.
- Mentors offer the benefits of their good practices, profound wisdom, and diverse experiences.
- Be discerning about whom you follow.

Takeaway Question

What do you envision your community group to look like to be most beneficial to you and for you to serve its members most effectively?

Applications: What Makes a Community Group Effective?

- Authenticity
    - Share the concerns, challenges, and choices that prevent you from moving forward in a mature walk with the Lord.
    - Recognize that there is no shame in confessing a sin or struggle.
    - Be the person you are rather than who you want people to think you are.
    - Do not be too eternally minded or use biblical babble when trying to instruct or encourage another—just be genuinely you!

- Loving well
    - Since life is relational, care for each member in your community group in a way that they know they can trust and count on you.
    - Speak with a tone of gentleness and tenderness that reflects a genuine love for the Lord and that just naturally covers the others in the group.
    - Show up with words of encouragement and outstretched arms to serve.
    - Be a good listener.
    - Forgive fully; do not rehash a resolved issue.
    - Hold each other accountable.

- Trust each other, celebrate with each other, and weep with each other.

- Humility
  - Confessing that you are a sinner and suffer from the same fallen state that affects each member of your community group creates a spirit of modesty, understanding, and mutual respect among all members.
  - Let others take up more time than is needed to discuss a concern, hurt, or prayer request even if it means you need to wait to share.
  - Accept the rebuke or insight of others with gratitude.

- Commitment
  - Be at the community group meetings on time.
  - Do any homework assignment that is required.
  - Attend community group consistently by making it a priority.
  - Offer to host or help with the arrangements.
  - Remain engaged in the group and be honest if topics or discussions challenge you or might offer differing viewpoints to your own.
  - Participate in activities together beyond the days and times you meet.

- Compassion
  - Show acceptance and welcome to all members.
  - Text or email members inspirational devotionals or messages that will encourage members who are struggling or challenged in areas of their lives.

- Everyone makes mistakes, falls short, and messes up, so embrace those who confess their sins.

- Honesty
    - If rebuking needs to be done, do it ... but do it in love.
    - Be transparent in sharing your own hurts and share them fully.
    - Keep confidential all that is discussed in the group meetings; remember, what is said in the community group *stays* in the community group!
    - If something is being discussed that does not reflect the truth of the Gospel or contradicts a biblical standard, quickly address that issue and correct it.

- Prayer
    - Open and close each time together in prayer.
    - Pray fervently for your community group members ... daily!
    - Pray some more.
    - Keep praying!

A friend loves at all times.

(Proverbs 17:17)

CHAPTER 5

RESTORING RELATIONSHIPS

Definitions

Relationships are God's most precious gift to us this side of heaven. It is people who matter in our lives. Family. Friends. The fellowship of those with whom you work, play, and worship. People who celebrate the victories and joys of life and who weep with you in times of sadness and heartaches. Our mental and emotional health thrive on the conditions of our strong relationships and flounder when we are out of sorts with important people in our lives. God wants us to live in unity with one another and knows being estranged or conflicted with others disrupts this harmony.

Yet you and I do things that wound others. Sometimes they are accidental, and sometimes they are intentional. Sometimes you are not the cause of a volatile situation that has created a grievance in the first place. Other people can be part of the failure too. Circumstances out of your control or factors not your doing could have contributed to a lapse in judgment, a mistake, or the collapse that brought you to this place. But no matter the cause, you are in a bad place with a person. Your relationship is fractured. You need to get this situation resolved, reconciled, and restored. How do you do that?

Next Steps

You have recognized this breach falls on you to do something. If, in fact, you were responsible for the adversity, own your mistakes, repent, and make things right to those whom you offended. Yes, there are consequences to poor decisions (and who hasn't made them?), but seeking forgiveness from those you have hurt and maligned creates reconciliation and restoration. Owning your mistakes and making things right to those who have been wounded by your actions is what defines you—not your faults, errors, and failures. It takes courage to admit you were wrong or that the fault was yours. God commands you to make relational restitution with an offended individual. Remember, humility comes before honor. How you respond to any circumstance is what defines you, not the circumstance itself. Asking forgiveness is a step on the path to regaining wholeness.

We are fighting a real enemy, the devil, who seeks to harm us. Scripture says this "thief" has one job description: to "steal and kill and destroy" (John 10:10). He is described as a "murderer" and "the father of lies" (John 8:44). Scripture speaks to his devious nature: "Your enemy the devil prowls around like a roaring lion looking for someone to devour" (1 Peter 5:8). Be alert. Do not listen to his accusations, lies, and false pronouncements! Instead, our Father in heaven wants you to cast all your anxieties on Him, "because He cares for you" (1 Peter 5:7).

What Does God Say to Do?

Adam and Eve's arrogance and rebellion to do what they wanted to do apart from God's good plans for them changed the course of human history forever and got us into the mess we are in today. God provided for all their needs in the glorious Garden of Eden. His one request was that they not eat from the Tree of the Knowledge of Good and Evil, or they would surely die.

Succumbing to the devil's temptation to eat a piece of fruit from that forbidden tree ushered in that original act of defiance and alienation from God. They were expelled from the garden, which consequently produced a future of brokenness, pain, hardship, and death—the effects of which are harsh realities today. Sin, fueled by the devil, *always* seeks to separate us from God.

I am so joyful that this sad story did not end with God turning His face away from the people He created and their future descendants. Despite the disobedience, bad decisions, and flawed behavior of people over hundreds of generations that have resulted in broken relationships among one another and with the Lord Himself, God consistently loves His children. And He forgives them.

As sinners, you and I need God's forgiveness and salvation. However, God must punish sin, which leads to death and eternal separation from Him. Since God is a holy God, He cannot allow the filth, darkness, and decay of sin to enter His heaven and into His eternal presence.

Since the Bible says we have all sinned and fallen short of the glory of God, we would never be able to earn our way into heaven based on our own merits or good works because sin constantly manifests itself through our polluted thoughts, words, and deeds.

To demonstrate His forgiveness for our moral transgressions and personal failings, God sacrificed His own Son, Jesus Christ, who was perfect and blameless, to die in our place. In doing so, Jesus took the full fury of God's wrath for our filthy sins so we may receive, in turn, His righteousness. God's forgiveness lavished on us through the death of His Son on a cross saved us from eternal separation from Himself that sin causes. How thankful we are for God's merciful and compassionate forgiveness in dealing with our sin because we can't get it right on our own. God now beckons you to forgive others.

God is serious about forgiveness. His own sacrifice of His Son, Jesus Christ, was huge. He speaks clearly and firmly about His expectations of your forgiveness to those who have wronged you. "Bear with each other and forgive whatever grievances you may have against one another. Forgive as the Lord forgave you. And over all these virtues put on love, which binds them all together in perfect unity" (Colossians 3:13–14).

Forgiveness is an intentional act. God leaves you no margin for misinterpreting His objective here. God demands we forgive. His extreme act of forgiveness for your sins in the ultimate sacrifice of His beloved Son, Jesus Christ, requires you to forgive those who have offended or sinned against you. God's forgiveness is one of the characteristics that defines His great love for us. It should be ours as well.

Easier Said Than Done?

You might be thinking, *God is perfect, so He can forgive. Anything is easy for God.* Yes, God is holy, perfect, and splendid. He loves us with an everlasting love. But He also sets into motion some requirements you must follow. God will never demand you to engage in activities that will harm, damage, or malign you. To the contrary, what He asks you to do is for your own protection and greatest interest. Scripture says every good and perfect gift is from our unchangeable Father. He desires the best for you.

God, our Creator, models forgiveness and is not asking you to do what He has not done Himself. He forgave through a mighty sacrifice. He requires you to forgive as well. That means forgive people who have been dishonest, abusive, or maybe even downright cruel to you. Anyone who has offended you needs to be forgiven. You might not be able to say it to them in person because some may have died, some may have disappeared from your radar and cannot be located, or some may not be in your comfort zone to contact. If people are still abusive, threatening, or can cause you harm, you wisely want to stay away from them. Being in their presence is never prudent if it creates any possibility for physical or emotional injury. However, God requests you forgive them whether they are standing in front of you or not. That burden of unforgiveness must be lifted from you.

Jesus did the same as He forgave those who crucified Him. Jesus, as He was nailed to the cross during the hours prior to His death, said, "Father, forgive them, for they do not know what they are doing" (Luke 23:34). As he neared death, Jesus's response was supreme compassion and love. Though in deep torment and agony, Jesus was asking His Father to forgive His enemies!

I pause for a moment to put horrible suffering in shocking perspective. Cahleen Shrier, a professor of biology at Azusa Pacific University and a distinguished writer and speaker on the physiology of Christ's crucifixion, wrote, "Crucifixion was invented by the Persians between 300–400 B.C. It is quite possibly the most painful death ever invented by humankind. The English language derives the word 'excruciating' from crucifixion, acknowledging it as a form of slow, painful suffering."[23] This sobering information requires taking a deep breath right now.

Yet in the midst of such unspeakable pain and misery, Jesus was asking God to forgive the soldiers who had whipped him, insulted him, put a crown of thorns on His head, and nailed Him to the cross. He was asking God to forgive His petty accusers and the mob who mocked Him, spit on Him, and hurled insults at Him. Jesus was willing to forgive His enemies and appealed to the outrageous grace of His merciful Father, whose plan for humanity's eternal salvation was anchored in forgiveness and rooted in Jesus's excruciating death on the cross. Jesus was born to die for our sins, and He interceded for His enemies while he hung on a cross. On the Sermon on the Mount, Jesus taught, "You have heard that it was said, 'Love your neighbor and hate your enemy.' But I tell you: Love your enemies and pray for those who persecute you" (Matthew 5:43–44). On the cross, Jesus, the One persecuted, was praying for His persecutors. God, the One with the plan, was demonstrating severe mercy and deep forgiveness for sinful humanity through His Son's death on that cross.

History is full of stories of people who have looked beyond their own misery, devastation, and the cruelty perpetrated on them by others to reach out and forgive them. During World War II, Corrie ten Boom and her family orchestrated a network to hide Jewish fugitives hunted by the Nazis. On February 28, 1944, the ten Booms were arrested, and Corrie was sent with her sister Betsie to the Ravensbrück concentration camp. Betsie died there, but Corrie survived.

In 1947, soon after the war ended, Corrie was speaking at a church in Munich on the topic of God's forgiveness. After her speech, Corrie came face-to-face with one of the guards who had been at Ravensbrück. He stuck out his hand and asked for her forgiveness. Corrie recalls the agony of what seemed to her like hours in the few seconds she stared at his outstretched hand. Her mind raced back to the cruelties and barbarisms of the concentration camp, including the death of her sweet sister. In her own words, she thought,

> I had to do it—I knew that. The message that God forgives has a prior condition: that we forgive those who have injured us. "If you do not forgive men their trespasses," Jesus says, "neither will your Father in heaven forgive your trespasses." ... Since the end of the war, I had had a home in Holland for victims of Nazi brutality. Those who were able to forgive their former enemies were able also to return to the outside world and rebuild their lives, no matter what the physical scars. Those who nursed their bitterness remained invalids. It was as simple and as horrible as that.[24]

Unforgiveness: An Effective Tool of the Devil

My friend, an unforgiving heart can harbor anger, resentment, or bitterness. Those emotions are like cancer, which seeks to destroy. As Bible teacher Beth Moore states, "Forgiveness may be excruciating for a moment … anger and bitterness are excruciating for a lifetime."[25]

Unforgiveness is a tool the devil effectively uses to restrict joy and diminish fulfillment. The intentional act of forgiving others releases the burden of dark, ugly emotions and replaces them with peace and calm. Forgiveness is a deliberate and planned action no matter how you feel. As Corrie ten Boom said, "Forgiveness is an act of the will, and the will can function regardless of the temperature of the heart."[26]

Most importantly, forgiveness reconciles relationships. God's desire for unity and harmony in relationships can only be achieved when strained relationships are reconciled. Restoration can only happen when anger, tension, and division caused by past conflicts are resolved. God requires forgiveness because it heals the brokenhearted, returns what is lost, and mends what is shattered.

Romans 12:17–19, 21 describes God's instruction to properly react when you have been offended:

> Do not repay anyone evil for evil. Be careful to
> do what is right in the eyes of everybody. If it is
> possible, as far as it depends on you, live at peace
> with everyone. Do not take revenge, my friends, but
> leave room for God's wrath, for it is written: "It is mine
> to avenge; I will repay," says the Lord. … Do not be
> overcome by evil, but overcome evil with good.

God calls us to be at peace with our brethren. In His Sermon on the Mount, Jesus declared a blessing on those who were people of peace. "Blessed are the peacemakers, for they will be called sons of God" (Matthew 5:9). This call to a standard of moral conduct pleasing to God emphasizes the importance of living in harmony. That can only be obtained by reconciled relationships. Further, taking revenge or doubling down in returning one bad action for another is unacceptable in God's economy. Simply stated, you are not to judge others. Luke 6:37 speaks boldly: "Do not judge, and you will not be judged. Do not condemn, and you will not be condemned. Forgive, and you will be forgiven." God is clear that He will take care of any needed punishment or discipline. That is His responsibility. He is the Judge of all people and will have the final word.

As we know, a court of law, through our legal system, will administer judgment of innocence or guilt on a defendant and punishment for illegal actions. God, as the ultimate Judge, will oversee and distribute severe consequences to those whose poor decisions, corrupt behavior, and sinful ways have hurt, harmed, or even brutalized your life. Your role is to take the high road to honor and display the Word of God even amid discord or conflict. While you must discern right and wrong behavior, God mandates forgiving rather than condemning your offender. God will manage the outcome and dispense the consequences.

What about You?

People have offended you. Forgive them. But what if you have hurt someone? What if you have messed up a commitment? What if you have stepped over reasonable boundaries, said something unkind, or caused frustration, distrust, or resentment to swell in someone's heart?

Whether intentional or accidental, have your actions in any way broken the bonds of a relationship? Offer no excuses. Own the mistake. Fess up. Ask forgiveness.

There is no substitute for humbly requesting forgiveness. It defuses anger and allows for healing to begin. Hurting another person, either willfully or accidentally, requires immediate action to repair what has been broken physically, emotionally, or spiritually. Go immediately to the person you have wronged to ask his or her forgiveness and repent of your infraction. If possible, do not let tomorrow dawn without taking care of asking forgiveness. Your mistake can fester inside someone's heart and dissolve a relationship if you don't swiftly own your transgression and make things right with another. The very heart of the Gospel message rests on the forgiveness of sins through the death of Jesus—God's plan, through His abundant grace, to save the world. Jesus is the model of One who forgave completely and sacrificially.

Forgiveness cannot wait. Let no unreconciled relationship linger. Resolve all personal estrangements, conflicts, and breaches. God's Word is crystal clear about this: "'In your anger do not sin': Do not let the sun go down while you are still angry, and do not give the devil a foothold" (Ephesians 4:26–27). Sin is an assault against the unity Jesus's sacrifice provides you.

Anger can unravel that harmony in relationships, causing tongues to slip and actions to destroy. Ephesians 4:26–27 uses one full sentence cautioning us not to let our anger outlast a day because that gives the enemy a grip to create havoc and disintegrate relationships. Apostle Paul wrote that message in a sentence in Ephesians, as if to imply the action of one is the necessary result of the other. Unresolved anger results in the devil's taking unwelcomed space in our lives through ruptures in relationships!

Do you need to forgive someone, or do you need to ask for forgiveness? Please make it a top priority … *today!*

Complete Forgiveness

If a person repents and asks you to forgive them, your forgiveness needs to be complete.

Yes, complete! When you forgive someone, whether it is a minor infraction or a big bruising transgression, that forgiveness needs to be final. Don't revisit it days, months, or years later. Forgiveness needs to be final when it is given.

When you ask God for forgiveness for a wrongdoing, aren't you glad He fully forgives you and doesn't keep bringing it up again? He doesn't remind you continually of your sin history. He throws away that sin memory and forgets it.

When God forgives you, He provides a special pledge:

> As far as the east is from the west, so far has he
> removed our transgressions from us. (Psalm 103:12)

Once you repent, God's forgiveness of your sins to the point of not recalling them again will be complete for eternity:

> For I will forgive their wickedness and will remember
> their sins no more. (Hebrews 8:12)

Oh, the peace of knowing God forgives you fully and will not dredge up the memory of your sins over and over. They are forgotten. They are gone! As Psalm 103:4 reminds us, the Lord "redeems your life from the pit and crowns you with love and compassion." Truly, God is abounding in His love for those who trust Him and who are faithful in following His written and revealed directives that lead to blessedness.

What joy grasping the sweetness that God fully forgives and forgets the sins of repentant believers! In turn, however, He expects no less of you.

Mimicking His forgiveness, you must guarantee that same grace when you forgive someone of their wrongdoing. That forgiveness *must* be complete. It is not to be revisited. The offender must be fully acquitted in your forgiveness. With your finite mind, you may still remember the transgression, but it is to be buried and not exhumed. A vengeful mind is not acceptable to the Lord, for He, and He alone, has the right to take revenge. Romans 12:19 emphasizes that truth: "Do not take revenge, my friends, but leave room for God's wrath, for it is written: 'It is mine to avenge; I will repay,' says the Lord."

Please hear this! You are to completely forgive as God, the King of kings and the Creator of the universe, forgives you. Like Him, pardoning another must be total and binding, not changeable and capricious. There is no room to hold on to a transgression that wronged you. You must forgive the offender fully and not bring it up months or years later. God does not do that and expects you to fully forgive as well. One of the most divisive characteristics in any relationship is digging up old hurts, reminding friends and family of their past mistakes or faults that led to brokenness in your relationship, and stirring up old accusations that were long ago dealt with and buried. This ungodly action creates resentment, tension, and distrust in any relationship. The enemy just loves old hurts to be unexpectedly unearthed and for one party to use that to punish the other. Conflict and a breach in the relationship are the natural consequences.

Most importantly, it is directly contrary to the way God has modeled forgiveness. As a reminder, God is clear about His view of forgiveness. Jesus says in Matthew 6:14, "If you forgive men when they sin against you, your heavenly Father will also forgive you. But if you do not forgive men their sins, your Father will not forgive your sins." The one who cannot forgive will not be forgiven.

Dear friends, that verse can be haunting. God mandates forgiveness. It could not be clearer. You are to forgive … and to forgive completely. God forgives those who forgive others. It will not go well for you to harbor unforgiveness and condemnation in your heart. The Gospel gravitates around God's forgiveness of you and me through the sacrifice of His precious Son. God expressed the importance of forgiveness and expects nothing less from you and me as well. Do you have any unreconciled relationship? Go and restore it in obedience to God's Word.

Perhaps the Hardest Thing—Forgiving Yourself

OK. You know God desires you to be in unity and harmony with others and to forgive them of their past grievances to you. Similarly, you need to go and be forgiven by others for any offensives you have committed against them. Restoration must be made for full reconciliation to be complete. But what about forgiving yourself? Are you walking with a soul that is heavily burdened because of a past that is dark or messy or compromised? Have you judged yourself with loathing and shame? Have you forgiven others, but you cannot forgive yourself? Scripture has a word for you: "Therefore, there is now no condemnation for those who are in Christ Jesus" (Romans 8:1).

God is our Judge. Throughout the Bible, He is referred to as the Judge who is given the responsibility to judge humanity for eternal purposes.

> But it is God who judges: He brings one down, he exalts another. (Psalm 75:7)

> Now there is in store for me the crown of righteousness, which the Lord, the righteous Judge, will award to me on that day—and not only to me, but also to all who have longed for his appearing. (2 Timothy 4:8)

It is the Lord who judges me. (1 Corinthians 4:4)

As your Judge and the Judge of all humanity, God has acquitted you of your guilt through the blood of His Son, Jesus Christ—a bold and unparalleled sacrifice that the divine Judge made so that you could be held blameless and righteous in His eyes and could pass through the gates of heaven when you breathe your last breath on earth. You are declared not guilty to the tyranny of sin because "the blood of Jesus, his Son, purifies us from all sin" (1 John 1:7). In an unbelievable move to show His love, God, as Judge, has forgiven our sins and has declared humanity not guilty even though we are unworthy recipients of that unmerited favor. Through God's outrageous grace, you and I receive the gift of eternal life He offers through faith in His Son, Jesus Christ. I still marvel at God's abundant love for us, and His desire to usher us into heaven. The King of kings wants to commune with us for eternity. Such love! Such forgiveness! Such sacrifice!

So that begs the question: If God forgives you, then why would you not forgive yourself? Why are you a dead person walking when God loves you beyond measure? The Bible is full of murderers, idolaters, adulterers, harlots, and deceivers who repented and whom God used for amazing Kingdom work. Drug addicts, felons, and cheats, once redeemed, have had beautiful places of use in God's economy today. Brokenness abounds in a fallen world.

I have never met a person with a pulse who does not have a story of some heartache, difficulty, or mistake that caused him or her to suffer at some point in life. That is why we need Jesus! We are prideful, selfish, and stiff-necked people desperately in need of a Savior, and God sent One to die for our sins. There is no greater outreach of love and forgiveness. Again, I ask you, if God the Judge pardons you from your guilty sentence through the great sacrifice of His Son, then why would you not cherish that freedom? Why would you still choose imprisonment of self-deprecation, criticism, and scorn? Why would you let your own accusation and guilty pronouncement define you and hold you hostage? Be at peace. You are released! You are free!

God does not want performance robots. He wants you—complete with your hang-ups, bang-ups, and hiccups! Come as you are. Be easy on yourself. Repent. God is calling you to forgive yourself and walk in the joy of His strength, mercy, and compassion.

Prayer—God's Powerful Tool

Years ago, when Bob and I were newly married, we were on our way to an event, and the traffic slowed down. Soon, we came upon an accident. The ambulance's red lights were pulsating against a dark night, and we could see the gnarled forms of a few cars. Bob quickly said that we must pray for the people involved whenever we pass an accident. Today, whenever I see an accident, I start praying immediately.

How many times I have prayed for those who are sick, anxious, scared, lonely, despairing, confused, and lost. I know the power of prayer, for I have been the recipient of thousands of prayers over many decades during heartbroken times in my life. My own fervent prayers have covered my family, friends, and myself as well as strangers both on domestic soil and in countries thousands of miles away with words of celebration and praise to God for victories achieved and, conversely, with impassioned pleas for mercy, calm, peace, justice, and healing. How I have lifted up petitions for God to intercede in the lives of those who don't know Him! I am continually reminded that prayer is God's tool for getting His work done.

Bob shared with me that God answers prayers in four ways.

First: "No, I love you too much." God wants the very best for you, dear one. He has such a great plan for your life, but many times your prayers are for so much less than what God wants to provide for you. Your requests may even be harmful, destructive, or risky without you realizing it. He doesn't want to give you mediocrity. He wants to lavish you with so much more.

Second: "No, not yet." You can ask for something but maybe not be equipped enough, mature enough, or wise enough to receive it. God knows the perfect timing, though sometimes it's far different from your ticking clock, to shower you with His blessings. How much better are God's plans for you than what you have requested! His delay does not mean His denial in providing for you.

Third: "Yes, I thought you would never ask." Oh, how God wants to communicate with you! Bring your heartfelt joys, sorrows, laments, and disappointments to Him in prayer. He wants to hear from you. Remember, God knows your every thought but wants you to tell it to Him! He has an answer for you. Prayer is the environment in which God transforms you. The fulfillment of His great plans for you begins and continues with prayer.

Fourth: "Yes, and here's more!" Such a sweet victory! Outcomes immeasurably more than you could have asked or imagined! God's goodness and love poured out as you experience the astounding awe and joy of His answer to prayer!

Yes, prayer matters to God. It is a mighty weapon in your arsenal to use effectively in moving forward in love, freedom, and forgiveness. God provides wisdom, clarity, and strength when we take our petitions to Him.

The Toughest of Prayers

God instructs you to pray:

Pray continually. (1 Thessalonians 5:17)

> Then you will call upon me and come and pray to
> me, and I will listen to you. You will seek me and find
> me when you seek me with all your heart.
> (Jeremiah 29:12–13)

God also requires you to pray for those who hurt you, harm you, and hate you. Jesus said:

> But I tell you who hear me: Love your enemies, do
> good to those who hate you, bless those who curse
> you, pray for those who mistreat you. (Luke 6:27–28)

That's a tall order! It is hard to pray for a person who has willfully betrayed you, violently harmed you, or even taken the life of a loved one. That seems like too much for Jesus to ask. But you must remember that Jesus died for them too. In God's economy, every life is precious and worth saving. There is consequence for sin, and everyone who has done unspeakable damage or caused gaping holes in your heart will have to answer to the one true Judge. God's wrath is not pretty and will heap punishment on the offender that will be quite dreadful. You might not ever see that happen, but God does judge firmly. You can count on that! It is not your responsibility to pronounce guilt but, rather, to do everything you can to resolve the offense in a manner pleasing to God. If it cannot be resolved, you leave that outcome to God's judgment, and you pray for the offender. You must pray for *anyone,* including those who have hurt you. You must pray that their hearts will be changed and that, if possible, given the circumstances, you will be able to be reconciled to them. It takes courage, faith, and determination to reconcile with others. But you must do everything possible to restore all relationships before you breathe your last breath. To that end, it means forgiving a person even if you are never able to show them that grace in person.

Forgiveness releases you from bitterness, anger, and agitation that the enemy so easily entangles in your life. Do not give the devil that foothold and entrance into the crevices of your heart! Forgive and pray for your enemy or anyone who has not had your best interests at heart ... even those who have maligned you. Forgiveness is freeing when you lay your prayers at God's throne of grace.

Chapter Summary Points

- The very heart of the Gospel message is God's forgiveness of our sins.
- Forgiveness is an intentional act.
- God demands we forgive others.
- God's Word clearly says if you don't forgive the sins of others, then God can't forgive your sins.
- Reconcile your relationships immediately!
- Forgiveness of an offense needs to be resolved completely and not be continually revisited or exhumed later.
- As the ultimate Judge, God's pardon of your guilt through the blood of Jesus releases you from anything that prevents you from forgiving yourself.
- Pray continually for those in your life, including those who have hurt or harmed you.

Takeaway Question

How do you plan to specifically reconcile a currently derailed relationship, forgive someone who has committed an offense against you, or ask someone whom you have wronged for forgiveness?

Applications: Ways to Reconcile Your Relationships with Others

- Identify any person(s) with whom you need to ask forgiveness and/or to reconcile a relationship.
  - Include any individual(s) with whom you have not fully resolved a conflict.
  - Discern how those relationships soured and your involvement in that decline.
  - Recognize ways the enemy has further distorted the conflict to the offended party(s) to be sensitive in how to respond.

- Initiate a plan to restore a broken relationship.
  - Seek the appropriate communication with that person.
  - Own your responsibility in the offense.

- Confess your role that created the disconnect or brokenness.

- Accept your responsibility in the fractured relationship.
  - Speak with sincerity, humility, and authenticity as you seek forgiveness.
  - Follow up with that person to demonstrate your commitment to the relationship if the purpose is to mend the relationship and continue it.
  - If your goal is to seek forgiveness only, be humble in asking for forgiveness and offer to do what is necessary to rectify the transgression.
  - Be accountable to do whatever is needed to restore the relationship.

- Pray specifically for the person whom you have wronged or who has wronged you and that reconciliation will take place.

- Undertake a personal audit to understand how you both got entangled. Examine your heart to fully understand where you have tendencies to hurt people, say things that should not be said, or react in ways that can easily deteriorate relationships.

- Be honest and candid with yourself as you scrutinize consistent behavior you display in certain circumstances that can lead to destructive or abusive actions against another.

- Pray that the Lord reveals those tendencies, and actively pursue ways to avoid and delete that behavior from your life.

- Ask a trusted person to be your accountability partner to help direct your steps to forge healthy habits and behaviors that eliminate destructive tendencies to damage relationships.

- If necessary, enroll in a program or seek professional counseling that will help you find solutions to combat and improve those divisive inclinations that wound others and destroy relationships.
  - Classes at local churches specializing in strengthening, repairing, or building relationships.
  - Anger management classes.
  - Interpersonal relationship classes.

Get rid of all bitterness, rage and anger, brawling and
slander, along with every form of malice. Be kind and
compassionate to one another, forgiving each other, just
as in Christ God forgave you.

(Ephesians 4:31–32)

CHAPTER 6

RESTORING COMPASSION

Attendance versus No-Shows

Being in crisis is an interesting phenomenon. It is a filter through which you experience the support of friends. Like a sieve, tragedy reveals the purity of friendship. Disaster, in all its shapes and sizes, exposes the depth of your relationships.

For the three years Bob was sick, we were buoyed by the depth and breadth of people's concern for us, demonstrated by their acts of kindness. So many helped us move forward. We loved these friends and had done the same for them when they were in difficult places. That is what friends do for one another; they serve, comfort, and encourage in times of joy and sorrow. We were so grateful when our friends showed up to help.

What surprised us were the many who showed up who we never expected to help. They were beautiful people whom we knew but not well, certainly not to expect such thoughtfulness.

Their care was a glorious blessing to us and deepened these friendships.

What also surprised us were those we knew, broke bread with, and shared life with who did not come around to offer a word of encouragement or offer to help. However, I wasn't hurt or angry. There was no feeling of betrayal nor condemnation. I was too busy doing battle with a vicious disease. But I was just perplexed.

What Does God Say to Do?

The Bible chronicles suffering—from our expulsion from the Garden of Eden to the first murder, of Abel by his brother Cain. To the wars and destruction chronicled under bad kings and their leadership. To man's inhumanity to man caused by the greed, idolatry, and brutality of people who strayed from God. To the crucifixion of the Son of God on a cross, who came to die for this fallen humanity. We read of the trials suffered by people in both the Old Testament and the New Testament. In fact, suffering has endured throughout the ages, and so much of what was revealed in the Bible mirrors today.

Our civilization has become modernized and technology savvy with accessibility to tools, techniques, and toys that have rapidly advanced our abilities to work, operate, and live.

However, these things have not decreased suffering. In some ways, they have only progressed it. So how are we to react to all this suffering … particularly when it affects our loved ones and those around us?

Second Corinthians 1:3–4 tackles this question:

> Praise be to the God and Father of our Lord Jesus
> Christ, the Father of compassion and the God of all
> comfort, who comforts us in all our troubles, so that
> we can comfort those in any trouble with the comfort
> we ourselves have received from God.

That is a call to action from God. As the God of all comfort, who has been a source of compassion, mercy, and steadfast love in your times of need, He has now summoned you to share His comfort with a hurting world. You have encountered over and over again the goodness of God's kindness and faithfulness when you were in desperate need. He has redeemed you, rescued you, and refreshed you. Time and again, He has lifted your sorrows and soothed your broken heart with His unlimited compassion.

Now God beckons you to extend that same reassurance, encouragement, and consolation to others because of what He has done for you. He calls you to serve others. His comfort flows to you in your sufferings so you, in turn, will comfort others in their distress. His grace to you is intended to be shown and not hidden. Indeed, God provides His tender mercies and steadfast love through the service of His people. You and I, therefore, are called to serve others.

My friend, as a reminder, all that you have—every talent, every material possession, every comfort—is because God first gave it to you. The very heart beating inside you is only beating because God put it there. Serving others is an act of worship. You are not called to insulate your gifts and talents but to infiltrate them into the lives of others.

One More Thing

God's call to a standard of living is found in Colossians 3:12–14: "Therefore, as God's chosen people, holy and dearly loved, clothe yourselves with compassion, kindness, humility, gentleness and patience. Bear with each other and forgive whatever grievances you may have against one another. Forgive as the Lord forgave you. And over all these virtues put on love, which binds them all together in perfect unity."

If you have a pulse and heartbeat, you have a responsibility to be relentless in your pursuit of kindness, care, and thoughtfulness toward others. That is just the right thing to do! It is important to respect others and have compassion for them, forgiving them and loving them through their brokenness and flaws. Particularly if you follow Jesus, it is your calling to live and embrace these standards of godly living. Serving others is the most demonstrative way of reflecting Christlike qualities.

Jesus delivered a judgment parable about service in Matthew 25:31–40. He said those who fed the hungry, gave drink to the thirsty, welcomed strangers into their world, clothed the poor, cared for the sick, and visited those in prison did it for Him. In this parable, Jesus was referring to the very neediest people with the lowest socioeconomic status. He was emphasizing the importance of compassionately serving others without expecting a reward or anything in return.

Instead, you serve out of kindness, sacrifice, and grace just as Jesus did Himself.

Love is what defines God. He is the Creator of love. His language is love. Matthew 22:37–39 quotes Jesus on what are the two most important commandments:

> "Love the Lord your God with all your heart and with all your soul and with all your mind." This is the first and greatest commandment. And the second is like it: "Love your neighbor as yourself."

So Jesus has showed us what He wants us to do—love Him and love others. Pretty simple theology but not always easy to execute. He doesn't care how we do it, but He cares that we, in fact, love intentionally and lavishly. That's the way He loves us.

Can you imagine what our world would look like if people did that? If people put others first rather than being self-seeking and dedicated to their own personal agendas, awards, and return on investments? When the joy of helping others was fulfilling enough? When pouring more of one's resources into humanitarian aid took center stage to building the size of one's audience?

Service is an other-focused action rather than a self-focused one. When making your to-do list for the day, include making a call to someone who could use a word of encouragement or a quick visit over homemade cinnamon rolls and hot tea.

Assign Yourself!

A very intelligent and well-respected friend of mine was sharing a lesson she learned from her late grandmother. Raised in the Deep South, this strong Black grandmother had survived miserable prejudices growing up and had endured discrimination and unfair treatment. However, she was resilient to such cruelties. She was a woman of great faith, unwavering determination, and tremendous wisdom. Her granddaughter, a distinguished educator at a respected university, told me she had asked her grandmother once to let her know how she could help her grandmother during an illness she was battling. The grandmother looked at her firmly and said, "Don't ask me when you can help. *Assign yourself!*"

What sensible and good theology! Assign yourself. We must take the initiative to reach out to those in pain. Those who are hurting. Those who are reeling from loss, hardship, or tragedy. Those who are discouraged, lonely, or grieving. Candidly, anyone who just needs *someone* to listen. Don't wait for the invitation; you probably won't get one. Suffering people are just trying to survive. Assign yourself.

Bob, William, and I lived at the hospital during the last three months of Bob's life since he was on a targeted clinical trial approved just for him by the FDA. He was doing so well on this trial until one week his body unexpectedly declined. It totally shut down. Within five days, Bob was gone. Brenda dropped everything from her home in San Francisco and came ready to help oversee the dozens of details that had just arrived unannounced with Bob's sudden passing.

The night before the memorial service, I sat at my computer at ten o'clock to write Bob's eulogy. Bob and I had planned his memorial service months earlier with our pastor, and my dear husband had asked me to speak at his service whenever that time would arise. I was honored to do that on behalf of our family. However, I had not expected this abrupt loss. I found myself exhausted and looking at a blank computer screen less than twelve hours before his service the next morning. As I began to write, I heard Brenda in the living room outside my office saying she was sitting down to read a book. I knew Brenda was as tired as I was and should be going to bed to face our big day tomorrow. She was not there to read. She recognized my desperation and anguish as this huge writing assignment loomed and my body, mind, and soul were totally depleted. Brenda assigned herself to be my sentinel, my advocate, and my supporter that evening, however long my writing took. During that lengthy night, I continually walked into the living room and asked her opinion when I got stuck in my writing. She would listen and gently respond as I read parts of my tribute to Bob. This went on for hours until I finished. Brenda stayed up half the night to make sure her heartbroken sister was comforted, encouraged, and prepared for the next morning. To make sure that I did not feel alone that very sorrowful and somber evening, she assigned herself to be present with selfless service and tender devotion. The eulogy, drenched with Brenda's loving-kindness and sacrifice, received a standing ovation the next morning.

Recognize you must assign yourself to be part of the rescue team. God rescued you from the brink of disaster. It is now your turn to assign yourself to help someone who is drowning in a sea of misery.

Just Be Present!

Candidly, it can be difficult to assign yourself to a friend who just lost a child. Or a coworker who just got laid off from her job. Or a comrade who was just served divorce papers. Life is so hard. Bad news comes like a speeding freight train out of control, flattening our friends and loved ones.

You think, *What could I possibly say to Cindy that would take away her pain of losing Bob? What could I possibly do to encourage William as he now faces his future without his dad?* Compassion is not necessarily a high-intensity action word. It can just mean sit and listen.

You might think you have to say something profoundly wise that would take away the heartbroken pain one feels after losing the love of their life. However, nothing you say would bring that person back. You are not God. But you *can* sit with them and be quiet. Listen to their cries or cry with them. Hold their hand. Speak softly or don't speak at all. *Be present!* Just be with the bereaved and the hurting, through their good and bad days. Offer no judgment for what is said or how it is conveyed. Demonstrate how much you care by just showing up.

So many people abandon their friends when tragedy busts through the door because they feel they don't have anything to say. Please don't be one of those people! You don't have to be brilliant, philosophical, or profound. You just have to *be present!* Attendance is required!

Mourn with Those Who Mourn

Romans 12:15 defines compassion: "Rejoice with those who rejoice; mourn with those who mourn." When a friend or loved one is in crisis, they need compassionate, kind, and encouraging counsel to help ease the burden of their affliction. Grieve with those who grieve. Cry with those who cry. In the hours, days, or months of hardship, give grace to the one racked with anguish. Do not judge them. Their actions can be compromised by a despair that drills deep. When tragedy invades unexpectedly, sometimes knowledge, wisdom, and understanding can be shredded. Faith can be crippled when misery hovers unceasingly. Words and actions can be expressed that fall short of one's typical personality, discretion, and beliefs. Give those hurting room to grieve fairly without fear of prejudice or judgment.

Job, a man "blameless and upright" who feared God, addressed his friends who spoke false accusations and merciless condemnation against him when he was in great sorrow over having suddenly lost his family, wealth, and health. He said:

> A despairing man should have the devotion of his friends, even though he forsakes the fear of the Almighty. But my brothers are as undependable as intermittent streams, as the streams that overflow when darkened by thawing ice and swollen with melting snow, but that cease to flow in the dry season, and in the heat vanish from their channels. (Job 6:14–17)

You must discern that words spoken by someone in pain might not be in keeping with biblical truth or could be directed in anger against God … or even you! Suffering can reduce even the most devout person to a rubble of brokenness from which comes uncharacteristic remarks totally in conflict with their strong faith. Give them room to grieve. As a person of compassion, you must care for others by loving them well. Do not correct their words spoken from the depths of deep despair. Wait in silence and not rebuke. Show mercy rather than criticism.

Beloved pastor, seminary chancellor, and author John Piper assesses compassionate behavior in his popular 1993 article "When Words Are Wind." He says that people say things that they would not normally say when they are in seasons of grief and pain. Hastily uttered words spoken in distress do not indicate a lack of faith or passion for the Almighty. These words are for the wind and will be speedily blown away when the reality of the moment is not so desperate. Venting in despair does not mean a soul is embedded with darkness, evil, or disdain for God. Words spoken by one whose heart has been shattered during difficult times do not always fairly represent the true and faithful character of a person. Rather, they represent the real pain being felt during a temporary season of suffering that will pass. As the weight of the sorrowful circumstances lighten, the anguished person will be restored and may even regret the impulsive words. Dr. Piper encourages us to be compassionate and understanding of words expressed during these mournful times since they will typically be momentary and quickly blown away. These words, he writes, are "spoken not from the soul, but from the sore." He concludes, "If they are for the wind, let us wait in silence and not reprove. Restoring the soul, not reproving the sore, is the aim of our love."[27]

Silence Rules

Why is silence so hard to do? Is it the awkwardness of being in the company of someone, even looking eye to eye, with no audible sound being exchanged? Is it the desire to rush to say something, even if it is inappropriate or clumsy, so they know you are thinking of them? Is it because silence is sometimes viewed as a weakness because you are not in control or leading the conversation? Silence is a difficult thing to practice when in the company of others.

But what does God say about being still? Much!

Psalm 46:10 says, "Be still, and know that I am God."

The Hebrew word translated "be still" comes from the Hebrew word *raphah*, which means to be weak, to let go, or to release. Translated, this would mean "cause yourselves to let go" or "let yourselves become weak." When you surrender to God, you let everything go because God is sovereign and in control. You surrender to God's will in full trust.

Psalm 37:7 says, "Be still before the LORD and wait patiently for him."

As the Israelites were on the shore of the Red Sea trapped by Pharaoh's

Egyptian army moving in, they cried out to Moses, who answered their terrified screams in Exodus 14:13–14:

> Do not be afraid. Stand firm and you will see the
> deliverance the LORD will bring you today. The
> Egyptians you see today you will never see again. The
> LORD will fight for you; you need only to be still.

Being still means showing patience, trust, and submission. It means taking control out of your hands and putting it in God's. As Creator, God has a perfect plan and purpose for you when you allow Him to orchestrate it.

God uses silence to refocus your desire to control the situation to just *being* and letting Him work. By releasing the anxiety, you take time to be a comfort to others without the pressure of a defined outcome or an identified, tangible victory. You come prepared to trust the unknown to God. You are incapable of doing or saying anything that will change the dynamics of your friend's or loved one's situation, but just being present to cry or listen or pray will allow God's comfort, peace, and mercy to flow freely. You are the instrument through which God can work. After all, God uses people to get His work done. But that only happens when you put aside your own expectations and agendas for the moment and let God work through you. Be still and let Him control the situation. If you just show up, He can pour His abundant grace, hope, and mercy through you to bless the brokenhearted … even without you necessarily saying a word. Silence can roar when you assign yourself to be present!

God's Return on Investment

Return on investment (ROI)—the buzzword in financial markets. It's all about making money. You don't have to graduate from Harvard Business School to know that losing money on your investments is not what you set out to do! Being a good steward of the nickels and dimes that God has given you is not only wise but is mandatory to fulfilling your daily living needs.

Actually, God doesn't exactly see the outcome of investment quite that way. Yes, He has given you brains, discernment, and even good financial advisers to help you make wise investment decisions. But God's economy gauges things a little differently. God says invest in people even if you don't get an immediate return on their favor or support. Do the right thing even if it is sacrificial. Put in the time to encourage, sit with, and listen to someone needing support even if your bandwidth is severely limited. Compassion never counts the cost.

Sometimes doing the right thing causes you to lose someone's praise or even friendship because it is not politically correct or what everyone else is doing. Do it anyway! Chances are if everyone else is doing it, then it might not be the correct thing to do in the first place.

Doing what God wants you to do is typically different from what others want you to do.

Forgiving someone for an offense even if they don't acknowledge their blatant misstep, misspeak, or mistake is what God calls you to do. Giving up a free night to help encourage someone in a tough situation, no matter how tired you are, is what God calls you to do. Taking your family to impoverished places to build water wells, help with disaster relief, or minister to orphans rather than going on a more comfortable vacation could be what God calls you to do.

Doing the right thing never changes to wrong because it seems too hard, makes you less popular, or is inconvenient. It is the right thing even if you don't get the accolades that you would like or the appreciation you think you deserve.

God's definition of a return on investment might be far less than you receive from man's perspective, but it is a jackpot in His economy. It is about showing steadfast love, goodness, and kindness to people without any expectation of a returned reward that, instead, reflects the grace, mercy, and compassion of God. It is about glorifying God and not about bringing praise, recognition, or credit to yourself. Jesus defined His litmus test for mastering the skill of living in Matthew 25:40: "I tell you the truth, whatever you did for one of the least of these brothers of mine, you did for me." God's value system is quite different from ours. He clearly honors the heart of a compassionate person who helps the most vulnerable and disadvantaged.

What a Privilege ... and Blessing!

It is an honor to help others. There is a great privilege walking with others during a challenging time and being a source of encouragement, restoration, and renewal to them. In that way, you radiate the *hesed* of God. The Hebrew word *hesed* embodies the faithfulness, mercy, loyalty, goodness, steadfast love, and kindness of God. It signifies the enduring covenant love and forgiveness God has for His people despite their sin and rebellion. These are permanent attributes of God that you can seek to imitate in serving your community and family.

Micah 6:8 speaks to the importance of *hesed*:

> What does the LORD require of you? To act justly and
> to love mercy and to walk humbly with your God.

When you act in this comforting way to show mercy, devotion, and loving-kindness to others in need, you are blessing the one burdened and, in doing so, are being the hands and feet of Christ. You are ministering to the brokenness of another and mimicking the enduring love God has for His people.

Remember how you have been loved and cared for over the years by the person in distress—whether it is a parent, a dear friend, a loyal coworker, or a member in your community—it is now *your* turn to be the one who is giving back. That is a privilege. Be joyful in the opportunity to bring comfort, mercy, and loving-kindness to them as they have done to you in the past.

To go and serve others who are strangers in need is equally a blessing. We are drawn together in humanity. Every person has a story. Sometimes those stories get twisted because of circumstances beyond the person's control. Neither you nor I are immune from making poor decisions that could have landed us on the other side of the law, could have addicted us to dangerous substances, or could have lured us into abusive relationships. Only by God's outrageous grace are you and I spared. But others are not, and it is important we serve them because, in doing so, we are serving the King of kings. That is an honor and a privilege.

But this privilege of being faithful and merciful to those in despair requires action. It mandates you to reach out. Even when you are tired. Even when it is not convenient. Even when you had something else to do. Serving others is your duty. Rather than run away from the emergency, respond to it. Go. Sit. Listen.

Oh, the power of love and compassion! When God calls you to serve, your acts of mercy redeem the lost, mend the brokenhearted, and free those from physical, emotional, and spiritual bondage. Successful rescue missions save the condemned. In doing all this, God's goodness continues. In your act of service, God turns the tables. In blessing others, *you* are the one who is transformed. God's joy and favor rests on *you*. Ultimately, *you* are the recipient of the greatest blessings. *You* are the one changed! That is how God's economy works. What a great return on investment!

Chapter Summary Points

- You are called to comfort others in affliction the way God has comforted you.
- Serving others is an act of worship.
- Relentlessly showing mercy and kindness to those in need models God's lavish love for humanity.
- Serve others without expectations of receiving anything in return.
- Assign yourself to take the initiative and reach out to those suffering rather than wait to be asked.
- *Be present!* You can't change the shattering situation, but by showing up, you can be a source of great encouragement and hope without even saying a word.
- Follow God's prompting. He will use you to comfort and console when you surrender control to His leading in the situation.
- Allow people grace when they are grieving or struggling rather than judging what they say or do or rendering opinions that could be harsh, critical, or demeaning.
- God's economy of return on investment is relationship-centric and people focused, not financially driven.
- While your merciful efforts bless those who are suffering, you are the one who is transformed and who ultimately receives the greatest blessing!

Takeaway Question

What action can you consistently take to compassionately and willingly serve, encourage, or reach out to someone in crisis? Is there anything preventing you from doing that?

Applications: How Do You Effectively Respond to Someone Who Is Suffering?

- Commit to investing time to console, encourage, and be present for the person who is suffering.

- Determine how much time they need to get settled and catch their breath from the tragedy, loss, or difficult situation since different circumstances require different lapses of time.

- If possible, notify the individual that you would like to see them and set up a time to visit.

- If there is a funeral or memorial service involved, try to attend.

- Think of the ways you can help.
    - Oversee meal delivery.
    - Help with housework or yardwork.
    - Pick up children from school or take them to activities.
    - Assist in recording deliveries, notes, or food that is being sent for future correspondence of thanks by the grieving party.
    - Adhere a creatively made poster on the front door of the person's residence and have friends stop by and write notes of encouragement on it.

- Research grief, anger management, or other resource-based recovery organizations and therapies that would be critical for the person in need or their family members to access or attend.
- Identify other family members of the person directly affected (children, parents, siblings, etc.) and make sure their needs are met as well.

- Show up!
  - Be a friend! Be an encourager! Be visible!
  - Be a good listener.
  - Be on time.
  - Assess the energy level and emotional temperament of the person.
  - Let the person drive the conversation and express their grief, anger, confusion, or whatever emotions they are feeling.
  - Respond with sympathy, sincerity, and composure. You don't need to say something that will change the circumstance—because it can't be changed.
  - Unless you are a pastor, do not try to interpret God's plan in the situation or try to offer explanations.
  - Depending on the fatigue level, be sensitive to the length of your visit.
  - Give the person a journal to record his/her prayers, thoughts, and emotions.
  - Pray with and for that person when together (if that is appropriate) and for them throughout the day.

- Continue to be present.
    - As the days turn into weeks and months, continue to communicate, visit, and offer encouragement so the person does not become isolated.
    - Galvanize others to rally around the person to be sources of joy and compassion through constant connection.
    - Write encouraging notes on a regular basis or call if it is hard to be physically present.
    - Don't lose contact.

- Laugh together!
    - Laughter, as a positive sensation, is scientifically supported as a useful and healthy way to overcome the effects of stress and depression.[28]
    - Laughter therapy, as a nonpharmacological alternative treatment, provides positive effects on one's mental health and immune system; helps create healthy psychological, social, and physical relationships; and can improve quality of life.[29]

- Take them for walks.

- Spend five to fifteen minutes a few times weekly in direct sunlight, which increases the brain's release of serotonin and creates the following outcomes:
    - Increases vitamin D to reduce inflammation, modulates cell growth, and helps bones absorb calcium.
    - Improves mood, calm, and focus.
    - Provides more restful sleep.
    - Lowers blood pressure.[30]

- Continue to check in.
  - Keep in touch with the person.
  - Help that person reach out to others.
  - Monitor the person's involvement in the community, his/her mental health stability, and overall well-being.

Finally, all of you, be like-minded, be sympathetic, love one another, be compassionate and humble.

(1 Peter 3:8 NIV2011)

CHAPTER 7

RESTORING PURPOSE

Derailed Detours

A re you right now where you were expecting you would be five years ago? Ten years ago? Twenty years ago? Particularly if you are over forty, are you singing from the mountaintops? At forty-four, I never thought I would be on a cancer journey with my husband that would find me burying him three years later. That wasn't in my plans ... *ever!* So many people in their postforties were expecting joy, success, and accolades. Instead, they got sorrow, failures, and brokenness.

It wasn't supposed to be like this! God, what is the purpose in all this? What is my purpose in all this? Our emotions and faith are shredded as we cry out to God for help in a bewildered state of disbelief and aimlessness.

Life's journeys can be hard and unpredictable. The road can be bumpy. Plans can be easily derailed. The destination might not be as magical as we expected. Relationships can be strained or broken along the way.

But at the end of each laborious journey, we realize there were positive outcomes that made life more rewarding for ourselves and for others. We championed something, overcame something, or discovered something and were better for it. We can even say, if we are honest with ourselves, that many times we would do it all over again. The journey was tough, but the testing was designed for our own benefit, strength, and maturity. And, as importantly, there was good in it for others along the way! In essence, there was a purpose in all of it.

Can you imagine yourself saying that?

Even amid life's tough and messy journeys, God has a plan uniquely and wonderfully created just for you. From the moment you entered the world, you were wired with gifts, talents, and attributes that would equip you for a wondrous purpose that only belonged to you. Furthermore, God uses your heartbreaks, hurts, and hardships as your platform to encourage and bless others … for a greater good much bigger than yourself. You were made for this! Your circumstances, however muddled, chaotic, and difficult, help define your purpose.

Some of the biggest blessings in life can be found on the path of suffering.

What Does God Say to Do?

You are God's masterpiece. Ephesians 2:10 sums this up: "For we are God's workmanship, created in Christ Jesus to do good works, which God prepared in advance for us to do."

Friend, you have a job to do! Plans to keep! Tasks to fulfill! God, the Creator of all things, has an individual assignment just for you throughout this journey called life. Depending on the way He wired you with your many gifts and talents, God has a sovereign purpose for your life that is good and will lead to hope and redemption—and not just for you but for others. He does not want you to insulate yourself from the world but to *infiltrate* it. God wants you to share your story with others about the way He has used all the beautiful and ugly components of your life to mature you, grow you, and redeem you.

The Lord's rescue comes in all shapes and sizes. Maybe He reached down into a dark pit to pull you out of the filth, murkiness, and chaos you found yourself in. Maybe He uttered a constructive rebuke on behavior not acceptable to His standard of living. Maybe He allowed things to get worse before they got better to bring you to the end of yourself and finally realize that what you were doing was not going well for you. But that reroute from the path of destruction to the path of righteousness is part of your story and needs to be shared.

He reminds you that your association with some people needs to be reconsidered.

> Do not be misled: "Bad company corrupts good character." (1 Corinthians 15:33)

> He who walks with the wise grows wise, but a companion of fools suffers harm. (Proverbs 13:20)

He prompts you to choose your words carefully.

> Do not let any unwholesome talk come out of your mouths, but only what is helpful for building others up according to their needs, that it may benefit those who listen. (Ephesians 4:29)

The battle for control of your mind is mighty and fierce, as the enemy seeks to captivate it with thoughts that weaken God's plans and leave you vulnerable to poor decisions, discouragements, and disappointments. The enemy uses his sharp and effective tools to chisel away and try to destroy the work of art God has created you to be.

However, Galatians 6:9 reminds you that down the road, God has a beautiful harvest planned for you that will bless you. "Let us not become weary in doing good, for at the proper time we will reap a harvest if we do not give up." That harvest will bless others, my friend, as God uses your life story to be a source of great strength, inspiration, and help to a world in need. Your story is meant to be shared! It will bring forth great fruit in the lives of others who identify with your wanderings, share your anguishes, and weep with your grief. They will see the redemptive work God has done to restore your focus, faith, and family. They will marvel that you have overcome great obstacles and despair. They will watch you move forward with resolve despite being stuck so many times. They will see the light of the Redeemer through your transformed life.

You Are on a Mission!

Growing Leaders, an organization that analyzes and instills timely life skills and leadership principles into young adults, chronicled "Six Fears and Concerns of College Students Today." Topping this list was "They want their life to count," writes Dr. Tim Elmore.

"Nine out of ten of them think about the future several times a week. They desire a 'life of purpose' and want to engage in work with a higher meaning than to merely draw a paycheck. They're trying to make sense of it all, but life gives them an anxious eagerness about the future."[31]

I salute young adults for wanting to live out their purpose and for embracing a higher goal than just personal comfort. We must understand what we were created to do. We must make our life matter so that the next generation is better. Most of us want to pursue a calling rather than just a career. We want to feel our life counts. Do you?

But God

But God ... my favorite two words together in the English language. Life is all about God. We were designed to worship Him. As Psalm 29:2 says, "Ascribe to the LORD the glory due his name; worship the LORD in the splendor of his holiness." Everything that *is* has only happened because God has ordained it to happen. Every talent you have, every success you have experienced, and every joy that makes you squeal happens because of God's goodness and His love for you.

The gifts and talents you were wired with since birth weren't meant to be hidden but to be exercised and used. They frame your life work, your activities, and those things that are important to you. Your personal characteristics add depth to your story, influence your thinking, and impact your decisions. They define issues of integrity, commitment, and kindness. They speak of courage and discouragement, of joy and sorrow, of victory and defeat. Your story is as messy, dysfunctional, and flawed as it is triumphant, beautiful, and praiseworthy. Your actions can result in fist pumps and shouts of gladness or in dropping your chin to your chest in embarrassment, sadness, or disappointment. Oh, life can be so severe and tough! One moment you are singing from the mountaintops, and the next you are parched in the desert. And it's all wrapped up in the frames of the motion picture called *Your Life*.

But God ... He gets it. Even when life is hitting you with two-by-fours. He is your provider. Your safety net. Your refuge. Nothing surprises God. He has a plan and a purpose for you. Pain and suffering are part of that plan for your life story. It drives us back to Him. Nothing is wasted in God's economy! Not even the darkness of your past. God can work though messes. Unwise decisions, broken relationships, and shocking scandals *never* disqualify the strength and impact of your story and your credibility in sharing it.

God uses these woven episodes of your life for good. It is never too late to be used by God. You are just like every other person with a pulse—imperfect! That's just the nature of fallen humanity—broken, hurting, and in need of rescue. That is why the world so desperately needs a Savior! And that is why this Savior can so effectively use your story—to point people back to Him!

"But You Don't Know My Past!"

I may not, but God does. Your past is just that—your past. Don't let it define you or who you will become. Don't let it follow you. You don't live in that space anymore. You've closed the door behind you and left the past no forwarding address. Sure, the past happened. You can't change that. But you can use what the enemy meant for your woundedness and now use it for what God wants. That is, for your good and for the good of others. You and I serve a loving God who redeems and restores broken lives. He uses flawed histories to give hope to others. Your story, with your messy past, has power in it to bless others.

Irish poet and playwright Oscar Wilde wrote, "Every saint has a past, and every sinner has a future."[32] My friend, God is not done writing your story!

God uses sinful and damaged people to change the world. Three of the Bible's most respected and powerful leaders—Moses, David, and Paul—were men with dark pasts. All three were murderers.

David, the great and beloved second king in the ancient United Kingdom of Israel and Judah, known for his repentance and submission to God and from whose line Jesus comes, added adultery to his résumé. He was also a passive father who failed miserably in maintaining discipline among his arrogant and violent children, which created conflict and destruction within his family.

Paul is considered the most influential leader in the history of Christianity after Jesus, impacting the growth of the early Christian church and spreading the Gospel throughout the Roman Empire in the first century. Paul is credited with writing at least eight books of the New Testament, more than any other biblical writer. However, before becoming a tireless missionary championing Christianity, Paul's original name was Saul of Tarsus, and he was a member of the Jewish religious party known as Pharisees, who were tasked with upholding the sacred law of the Jews. Before his dramatic encounter with God on the road to Damascus and subsequent conversion to Christianity, Paul zealously imprisoned and persecuted Christians and sought to destroy the early church movement. He was present and gave approval to the stoning of Stephen, the first Christian martyr.

Moses closely interacted with God in ways no other person was privileged to do in biblical history. He led the Israelites out of bondage from Egypt, received the Ten Commandments from God that established the foundation for Jewish law, and wisely governed the Israelites as they lived in the desert for forty years. Earlier in his life, Moses had killed an Egyptian man and fled. Decades later, a rebellious act that disobeyed God's instruction in the desert barred him from entering the land of promise.

But God. He knew the hearts of these three men were faithful despite their troubled pasts, faults, and weaknesses. They were used for God's important and redemptive work. What an impact they had on biblical history—three men who were far less than perfect by anyone's standards. They were blemished like all of humankind, yet the Almighty used them well for His purposes to advance His Kingdom and to lead people and nations to worship.

He does the same for you and me. Have you ever cried out to God, "*What are You doing*? This world is wicked, corrupt, and dark! Your holy eyes certainly cannot tolerate such evilness! *Do something!*" My friend, God *is* doing something! He is using *you*! God has no Plan B. We are His plan to get His work done. It is only through God's grace, goodness, and provision that redemption happens, but He uses people as His instruments of change. You might be the only Bible that those around you ever read. That means He can use *your* story for radical results!

Your Best Is Enough

God has given you a special allotment of gifts and talents. Just for you. Use them for good to the very best of your abilities. When that is done, know that your very best is enough. It's a simple strategy but is sometimes hard to put into practice.

Sometimes I believed the self-inflicted lie that my best wasn't good enough. So I kept striving for a better result when what I had already done worked fine. It was the very best I could do and, quite candidly, all that my skill sets allowed me to do. But I kept trudging away to do better—to do more. I was exhausted with the wasted time and energy I pounded into my efforts, with no improved results whatsoever. Sound familiar?

Yes, go "all in" to do what you have felt impelled to do. However, accept that when you have done your best, that is enough! You don't have to keep pushing for others to accept you more. You don't have to keep attempting to do the impossible as a way to earn anyone's added affection or approval. As importantly, you don't have to strive for God to love you more. He is crazy about you and wants you to trust in Him for all you need. You don't have to work feverishly to win God's favor. He is a good Father who delights in His children and treats them as valued treasures—even when they fall woefully short. You can take such comfort knowing that your Father's love is not dependent on your performance but, instead, is given abundantly to you because you belong to Him!

God Is More Than Enough

Infuse this important note to self and park it in your soul: *your best efforts are always enough.* Period. But do be reminded that you are not designed to be enough … *on your own.* It is through God's grace that you are enough. God says in 2 Corinthians 12:9, "My grace is sufficient for you, for my power is made perfect in weakness." God's power shows up through your weakness.

You and I are made to be dependent on Him, not on ourselves. You and I are truly enough through God's provision and steadfast loving-kindness. He is well pleased with you and will deliver what it takes for you to have enough … and more than enough … the very best … for your every need. Even when you are running low.

You don't have to prove yourself anymore to God. The Scriptures say that your very best isn't good enough on your own merits, and your very worst doesn't disqualify you from the love of God. Jesus gave his life for that. You are good enough, my friend, because God is more than enough and loves you beyond what you can imagine. Put aside your self-sufficiency and strenuous striving. Lean into Him.

Follow Your Passion

God has given you a passion for something. It is what ignites that bigger purpose He has designed for you. He has created you with abundant talents. He has called you to look beyond yourself and to use those God-given gifts for His glory and for the good of others.

Stretch yourself. Do not be paralyzed in fear. Be bold, courageous, and adventurous. Step beyond your comfort zone. Will you make mistakes? Most assuredly. Will there be some ups and downs, ebbs and flows, wins and losses? Count on it!

Athletes don't win every game they play. Actors don't get every role for which they audition. We all fail at one time or another. It's what makes the victory so special. It is what defines excellence—learning from the loss. Don't let people or the enemy discourage you by saying you don't have what it takes to go the distance. Don't let them convince you that failure means you are not good enough to get the job done. That is a lie and many times is rooted in jealousy, deception, and pettiness. If that is what you were called to do, go after it. You will have what it takes when an opportunity ignites your passion.

My mother won all nine Grand Slam women's singles championships she entered from 1951 to 1954. She was a member of the US Wightman Cup team from 1951 through 1954, winning all seven of her matches those four years and helping lead the US team to victory. The Wightman Cup was a major international women's competition between the top British and American teams held annually from 1923 to 1989. That is an impressive string of victories!

But Mom did lose matches. I once asked her what was the most important match she ever played. She said it was one she *lost*! I was so shocked! She lost to Ann Bissell when she was ten in the finals of the first tournament she ever entered. Mom told me that her backhand had failed her miserably in that match. She then went to work relentlessly on her footwork, accuracy, and stroke techniques to improve that backhand weakness. A year later, she faced Ann Bissell in the finals of a big junior tournament in San Diego. This time, she won the match decisively!

But that victory is not the message of the story. Sports writers and tennis journalists agree that Mom's backhand was one of the best backhands in the history of women's tennis. Mom's loss to Ann Bissell at age ten had revealed the weakness of her backhand. She worked tirelessly to improve it, ultimately becoming the reigning women's world tennis champion for three years, armed with her astounding backhand weapon. Mom's early loss at age ten was her ultimate victory just a few years later.

Do not give up on your dream. Do not forsake your mission. Do not think that God cannot use you. He gave you specific gifts and talents and then combined them with a heartfelt passion to go out there and engage them. His plans for you are always good. Failure and loss are all part of the experience and, in so many situations, become the catalysts that propel you to even greater things. Do the best you can with what you have. That's all you can do, and that is good enough. God is not keeping score. He is not disappointed, angry, or disgusted when you falter.

He is standing with open arms to catch you when you fall. He just wants you to get on with your mission because He has designed you for a mighty purpose. Let's go!

You Are Entrusted with Much!

Bob's statement shocked me. In the middle of the night, with pain wreaking havoc in his cancer-ridden body, he spoke. "Sweetie pie, we should feel it a privilege that God thinks we are capable of handling this challenge." I was half-asleep, massaging Bob's aching back, when Bob uttered those words. His comment was so unexpected that I thought I was having an out-of-body experience! *What?* "Privilege" was not the word I would have used at that moment. Exhausted. Sad. Uncertain. Those were apt descriptions of how I was feeling. Yes, I trusted in God's providence, but I was feeling more like I had drawn the short straw on God's suffering list at that moment, and Bob and I were getting pummeled. I just didn't get it in my fatigued and battle-weary state at two thirty in the morning. Maybe when dawn arrived, I would be more enlightened!

But Bob was relentless and chatty in the middle of that night. He said that we needed to be faithful with what God had entrusted to us.

First Corinthians 4:2 states, "Now it is required that those who have been given a trust must prove faithful." This context implies that those who have been *given a trust* are like house managers or stewards who are worthy to be entrusted with important and sacred things. The word *faithful* in this verse refers to someone God has found trustworthy, reliable, dependable, true, and unfailing. In some verses, the word *found* is used rather than *proven* and is translated from the Greek word *eurisko,* which means to find or to discover through careful observation.

Rick Renner of Renner Ministries explains that the word *found* tells us that God is carefully observing us to see our actions and reactions. "He is watching to see how we treat people, how we respond to pressure, and whether we have the tenacity to stay on track when distractions try to thwart our obedience. Before He taps us on the shoulder to give us a new assignment, He carefully observes to see how well we have done with the last assignment. Did we do it as expected? Did we finish it completely, or did we leave parts of the assignment incomplete? Did we do it in a way that glorified the name of Jesus?"[33]

That night, Bob was saying God had confidence in our capability to testify to His glory and worship Him despite our grim circumstances. These were the best of times and the worst of times for us. We watched our future dreams be crushed with a probable outcome. We realistically embraced this but so desperately tried to avoid the heartbreaking reality. On the other hand, Bob and I had immense joy watching people seek the Lord and place their faith in Christ as they saw us bring God the glory. The Lord knew that we would stay steadfast, disciplined, and obedient to share our devotion to Him despite our suffering. What a privilege that God trusted our hope in Him!

We were amazed God chose the two of us with our missteps and miscues. However, God saw all our imperfections as a perfect backdrop to showcase His power and love. Bob and I were transformed by the mercy and grace of God. I have written in my Bible that grace is getting what you don't deserve, and mercy is not getting what you do deserve. God wants you to be obedient in seizing each situation strongly and courageously. You are not to withhold anything but, instead, pour yourself out to bear witness to the goodness, truth, and beauty of your holy God. In His timing and loving-kindness, God's outrageous grace will be lavished upon you, and you will experience true healing and joy.

God Is There to Help You

Years ago, I saw a comic strip that impacted me. The first frame of the cartoon was an eggshell. The second frame showed a crack in the eggshell. In the third frame, a little chick's head appeared out of the eggshell. Next frame, the little chick looked to the left. Next frame, the little chick looked to the right. The next frame, the little chick looked straight ahead. And in the last frame, the little chick pulled that eggshell back over its head!

Isn't that what happens? You look at your circumstances and the journey ahead with its collisions, detours, and delays. In doing so, the enemy has robbed you of your joy and the motivation to keep moving forward. You want to retreat and abandon your game plan! But, dear one, like the little chick, you looked to your left, to your right, and straight ahead, *but you forgot to look up!* God has not wavered in His great plans for you. He wants you to get back in the journey.

While you are to be faithful to this privilege with which God has entrusted you, realize you cannot effectively accomplish it without His help. Without the Lord directing your steps, life is going to be burdensome and not bear the most luscious fruit. It is like the hamster running with vigor on that wheel but going nowhere. Your job is to be obedient *in* what and *with* what God has given you. There is no pressure in performance because God is responsible for the outcome. He just wants your faithfulness.

Our cancer journey was difficult, but God revealed Himself to us through it and carried us. So many times, Bob's pain was off the Richter scale. He was miserable, and I knew it. But he offered our nurses, oncologists, and caretakers such words of encouragement and support. One of our hospital nurses just couldn't stand it because she knew Bob's extreme discomfort. Almost incredulously, she asked, "Mr. Simmons, Mr. Simmons, what do you have that gives you such strength? What do you have that gets you through this crisis?"

Bob's answer was so characteristically calm. "It is not *what* I have; it's *who* has me!" Bob, William, and I were hitching a ride with God all the time! It was a good place to be ... cradled in God's arms!

Hope Is Found Here

One last thing. It is God who gives life meaning. As Creator, He has made everything with purpose and for the enjoyment of those He created. You and I arrive with gifts as well as with limitations. At times, our greatest frustration is our own unrealistic expectations of trying to make things work that just aren't set up that way.

In Ecclesiastes 3:1, we read, "There is a time for everything, and a season for every activity under heaven" followed by a litany of contrasted activities that affect life: "a time to be born and a time to die" (v. 2), "a time to weep and a time to laugh" (v. 4), "a time to keep and a time to throw away" (v. 6), "a time to be silent and a time to speak" (v. 7). But then we read in Ecclesiastes 3:11: "He has made everything beautiful in its time." In other words, God's purposes and appointments have reasons and order to them and are to be accepted with patience and gratitude. God knows your limitations. He has plans for you in His own timing, and they will be beautiful. Trying to do it on your own or in conflict with God's plans only produces meaningless results.

Ecclesiastes 2:10–11 bears out this truth:

> I denied myself nothing my eyes desired; I refused
> my heart no pleasure. My heart took delight in all
> my work, and this was the reward for all my labor.
> Yet when I surveyed all that my hands had done
> and what I had toiled to achieve, everything was
> meaningless, a chasing after the wind; nothing was
> gained under the sun.

And the summary in Ecclesiastes 12:13: "Now all has been heard; here is the conclusion of the matter: Fear God and keep his commandments, for this is the whole duty of man."

If you follow God's commandments, it will go well with you. Your way of doing life will be radically transformed. Recognizing the importance of forgiveness, humility, and compassion, which are all attributes of godly living, will restore your relationships. Speaking words of encouragement rather than harshness, exercising self-control in your conduct, and faithfully guarding yourself against the temptations and deceitfulness of sin are steps in mastering the skill of godly living. Glorifying God brings harmony, joy, and contentment into your life rather than worshipping the things that don't satisfy for the long haul. Yes, there will still be trials, heartaches, and conflicts. However, hope flourishes when your trust is placed in Christ and not in yourself.

Let's Get Moving!

God has given you a purpose. You might be looking for it, or you might have found it. But it can be used mightily when it is shared with others. Even if your life has caused you to stumble and fall, lose your way, or get flattened, God is there to pick you up and receive you when you turn to

Him. If you are covered from head to toe with the muck and mire that bad associations, poor decisions, or out-of-your-control situations have hurled at you, God is there to clean you up and carry you forward.

And you *will* move forward. You can't make things happen by standing still or going backward. This designed purpose is yours! Don't just walk with it! Run!

Your story matters to God, and it is important to all who hear it. How your words of regaining wholeness, reconciling relationships, and persevering in extremely difficult circumstances can encourage others. God can use you to show a watching world it *is* possible to regain hope and joy. You can be a catalyst to help people reconnect with themselves, with others, and with God. Whether your story has drama or whether you have been spared from some of life's most difficult challenges, it was meant to be communicated with others. Most importantly, God's outrageous grace is meant to be showcased and not hidden in silence.

So let's get moving! God has great plans for you!

Chapter Summary Points

- You are God's workmanship.
- God has mighty plans for you.
- God wants you to share your story to inspire, strengthen, and encourage others.
- God can use your story even if it is flawed, messy, or blemished.
- It is never too late to be used by God.
- Don't let your past define you or who you will become.
- God uses people to get His work done and as instruments of change.
- The best you can do is enough, but God is more than enough.
- Your passion ignites the purpose God has designed for you.

- The plans and purposes of God cannot be effectively accomplished without His help.

Takeaway Question

How has God used your personal story and His designed plans for you to transform you, influence others, and glorify Him?

Applications: Promoting and Expanding Your Story

- Identify God's designed plans for your life.

- Pray consistently for wisdom, clarity, and direction to discern how you will be most effectively used in sharing your story with others.

- Journal the impact and the struggles of communicating God's plans for your life.
  - People your story is affecting and inspiring.
  - Ways God has used you.
  - Challenges you are facing.
  - The enemy's resistance.

- Ask trusted friends to undergird you in prayer and counsel.

- Mentor individuals whom your story touches.

- Continue to revise, strengthen, and broaden your story.
  - Identify groups that would be interested in your story.
  - Identify speaking opportunities.

- Identify print and broadcast media and social media platforms that could have an interest in promoting your story.
- Consider writing a blog that includes elements of your story to encourage people.

- Create a website or microsite with content that showcases the following:
  - Your personal testimony and those of people who are sharing their stories.
  - Successes you have had in using your life experiences to inspire others.
  - Videos that further support, create calls to action, and/or add a deeper dimension to the full communication of your story.

"For I know the plans I have for you," declares the Lord,
"plans to prosper you and not to harm you, plans to give
you hope and a future."

(Jeremiah 29:11)

SECTION 3

GOD'S RESTORATION PLAN

Serving Somebody

Bob Dylan won a Grammy Award for Best Rock Vocal Performance by a Male for his song "Gotta Serve Somebody." It was from his 1979 studio album *Slow Train Coming*. A few of the song's clever stanzas:

> You may be an ambassador to England or France
> You may like to gamble, you might like to dance
> You may be the heavyweight champion of the world
> You may be a socialite with a long string of pearls
>
> You may be a state trooper, you might be a young Turk
> You may be the head of some big TV network
> You may be rich or poor, you may be blind or lame
> You may be living in another country under another name
>
> Might like to wear cotton, might like to wear silk
> Might like to drink whiskey, might like to drink milk
> You might like to eat caviar, you might like to eat bread
> You may be sleeping on the floor, sleeping in a king-size bed

And then the refrain after each stanza:
> But you're gonna have to serve somebody, yes you
> are
> You're gonna have to serve somebody
> Well, it may be the devil or it may be the Lord
> But you're gonna have to serve somebody

Bob Dylan got it right! You and I were made to serve somebody. Who will it be? Will the desires of this world, with their profound pleasures, passions, and possessions, hold your heart captive? Or will surrendering your life to God and adhering to His standards be your calling? Jesus said in Matthew 6:24, "No one can serve two masters. Either you will hate the one and love the other, or you will be devoted to the one and despise the other" (NIV2011).

It is incompatible to love God and love the secular temptations of the world at the same time. Your will and affections drift in one direction or the other to choose whom you serve. You can serve only one master.

You can love so many things that bring you joy, inspire your heart, and match your interests. Life is beautiful, so it is meant to be enjoyed—to the fullest! You have been given talents and wired with emotions to seize opportunities and utilize them for your own good and for the good of others. Go get 'em! You have loved ones and friends in your life who really matter and make your soul soar. Guard those treasured relationships well! The question posed, however, is not about savoring these splendid moments and people in life. Ultimately, you must decide who owns your heart. Whose life playbook do you follow? Who do you credit for what you have? What forms the foundation for your values and for discerning the truth? The answer offers two choices: it's either the values of the world or the values of God. It's either the charms of the devil or the callings of God. Ultimately, it comes down to who your authority is: self (flesh) or Savior (God).

Whom do you serve?

What Does God Say to Do?

Psalm 29:2 says, "Ascribe to the LORD the glory due his name; worship the LORD in the splendor of his holiness."

We were made to worship God. The Bible contains hundreds of references to praising God for His enduring love, steadfast faithfulness, and glorious works. This worship, which takes place in the spirit or heart of a person, is profound gratitude and joyful praise to God for His abundant love, grace, and mercy toward humanity. It is a devoted reverence to our Father for His plan of redemption through His Son, Jesus Christ, who provides the way for eternal salvation.

Psalm 100 sings of the worship due the Lord:

> Shout for joy to the LORD, all the earth.
> Worship the LORD with gladness; come before him
> with joyful songs.
>   Know that the LORD is God. It is he who made us,
> and we are his; we are his people, the sheep of his
> pasture.
>   Enter his gates with thanksgiving and his courts
> with praise; give thanks to him and praise his name.
>   For the LORD is good and his love endures
> forever; his faithfulness continues through all
> generations.

The Lord does not take kindly to idolatry. He doesn't tolerate you worshipping anything or anyone above Him. God is the one true God, unequaled in any way, so He does not accept unfaithfulness. The first and second of the Ten Commandments given to Moses by God as the divine law for the nation of Israel dealt with the prohibition of idolatry. The first commandment in Exodus 20:3 says, "You shall have no other gods before me." The second commandment in Exodus 20:4–5 says, "You shall not make for yourself an idol in the form of anything in heaven above or on the earth beneath or in the waters below. You shall not bow down to them or worship them." God does not look favorably on people who rebel against Him through worshipping anything other than Him.

God is serious about this. The Old Testament is full of woeful consequences of nations and cities God judged and annihilated because of their pagan god worship and moral decay. The once-powerful Tyre, Damascus, Edom, Bethel, Gilgal, Nineveh, and Babylon were ultimately destroyed, victims of God's wrath and judgment. Judah was punished for its spiritual apostasy, lawlessness, and social corruption with the invasion and its subsequent capture by the brutal Babylonians in 597 BC.

Look at your checkbook, credit card statements, and bank account withdrawals to see where your treasures are stored and what occupies your time, support, and emotional bandwidth. Jesus said in Matthew 6:21, "For where your treasure is, there your heart will be also."

Jesus implores you to look at who and what gets your attention. Those things will be the center of your worship. Relationships, education, work, and entertainment are all important parts of your life to provide pleasure, security, and satisfaction. Endearing people can be messengers of hope, but they are not the Good News. They can be encouragers, but they are not the Author of love. They can be voices, but they are not the One who speaks. Whenever you allow the voice of a person to be louder than the voice of God in your life, you have disrespectfully elevated a human being over the one, true, living God.

In God's economy, you must not let anything or anyone be your idol. Nothing can crowd out the worship of the King of kings who gave these precious gifts to you in the first place. And He, unlike any living or inanimate object, is the only One who can provide you eternal life. He is the only One who can save your soul. He is the only One who can rebuild what sin has destroyed. He alone is worthy of your worship. Apart from Christ, let nothing dazzle you.

What or whom do you worship? Do you have any idols in your life that have priority over God?

One More Thought

How do you form your opinions or establish your value system? From friends? News media? Celebrities? Where do *they* get their information? Is what you receive that will form the basis of your thoughts, judgments, and faith anchored in truth that will bless and save you?

God is the Creator of the universe. No one taught, consulted with, or showed God how to fashion the intricacies of creation. He has no rival. Isaiah 40:12 asked, "Who has measured the waters in the hollow of his hand, or with the breadth of his hand marked off the heavens?" God, with His great power and mighty strength, brings forth the stars, calls each by name, and not one of them is missing (Isaiah 40:26). He never grows tired or weary (Isaiah 40:28) even though He never slumbers or sleeps (Psalm 121:4). In six days, He set the stars, moon, sun, and all of nature in motion.

God masterminded galaxies both known and unknown. A galaxy is defined as a vast collection of gas, dust, and billions of stars and their solar systems, all held together by gravity. To put it in perspective, Earth is one planet among eight planets in our solar system—one solar system among more than a hundred million other solar systems belonging to a singular galaxy called the Milky Way. How many other galaxies are there in the universe? Astrophysicists vary in their estimates, but an acceptable range is between one hundred and two hundred billion galaxies![34] I am trying to wrap my spinning head around that! The Milky Way is *one* galaxy among one hundred to two hundred *billion* galaxies unknown to the most brilliant minds studying the universe!

But God knows. He created them all! He knows their names! This same God, who is so infinite, powerful, and limitless, wants a relationship with you and me. Despite His vastness, He cares about the issues that keep you up at night, hurt your relationships, and rob you of your joy. Our holy and perfect God beckons you to enter into an authentic and secure relationship with Him. And why not? He's worthy of your trust, more than any other person, place, or thing.

Is there anything keeping you from doing that?

God Knows Us ... Fully ... and Still Loves Us ... Fully

Psalm 139:2–4 says God knows us. He knows when we sit and when we rise. He knows our thoughts from afar. He knows when we go out and when we lie down. He is familiar with all our ways. He even knows what we are going to say before a word is on our tongue. Now *that* is really knowing someone! But it doesn't stop there. If we go to the heavens or the very depths of this world, God is there in these two vertical extremes (Psalm 139:8). If we rise on the wings of the dawn or go to the far side of the sea, God's hand will guide us in these two horizontal extremes (Psalm 139:9–10). In other words, God's inescapable supervision is with us in all spatial reality and in all of creation.

But what is so amazing is that someone who knows *everything* about us loves us so completely! Even though we have done some unwise, shameful, embarrassing, hurtful, and mean-spirited things, God loves us ... fully. Zephaniah 3:17 says, "The LORD your God is with you, he is mighty to save. He will take great delight in you, he will quiet you with his love, he will rejoice over you with singing."

Can you believe that the Creator of the universe sings songs of praise about you and chuckles with delight over you? He is giddy with joy that you are His! He is absolutely crazy about you! There is no comma at the end of that verse that would read, "He will rejoice over you with singing, *except* when you tell lies, act foolishly, wound people, forget to forgive, spew profanities at others and at Him, worship material things, and continue to drown in your selfish insecurities." The period at the end of Zephaniah 3:17 captures His overwhelming love for you. God relishes you, my friend!

I'm so grateful God isn't a fickle father, loving His children one minute and then rejecting them the next when they do something reckless, arrogant, or dishonest. You and I would never feel confident in God's love if it were based on our performance or behavior. Thankfully, He is neither capricious nor impulsive. Instead, God loves you so completely! His love is unwavering and steadfast as He describes in Isaiah 54:10: "Though the mountains be shaken and the hills be removed, yet my unfailing love for you will not be shaken."

Do you believe that God loves you that much?

God Fixes What Is Broken

Bob could fix anything. He was a walking handyman around our home. When a toy was busted, an appliance didn't work, or a piece of something came undone, William would take the broken item to Bob and insist, "Daddy, pleeeez fix it!" William had full confidence in Bob's ability to repair whatever had become unhinged. His daddy would solve the problem. When William was three, we went to the circus, and he asked for a shiny red balloon, which we bought for him. He could not take his eyes off this red, rubbery sphere. He held it firmly so that it would not escape his grip and carried the balloon so carefully to his seat. Once seated, he just gazed at it. Then suddenly, the balloon popped. A pile of red rubble just fell in William's lap. He was distraught. But he reached out to Bob and said, "Daddy, pleeeez fix it!" Bob was so good at mending anything, but he was not capable of restoring this wreckage of red rubber.

But there *is* a Father who can fix *anything*. You can take your shattered dreams, fractured hearts, and biggest disappointments to God and say, "Daddy, pleeeez fix it!" He will mend what is broken, find what is lost, and claim what has been discarded. He, indeed, cares for you and will provide for you.

Perhaps you have been sad or perplexed about how you saw God respond to a situation or, worse yet, allowed something to happen. With a taut face and firm words, you declared, "God! God! *What are You doing?* I don't understand." It is fine to not understand God. His wisdom is immeasurable, limitless, and incalculable as compared to yours. He gives you total freedom to express your anger, confusion, and heartbreak to Him. He can take it!

But the danger is putting a period at the end of the sentence. "God! God! I don't understand."

The escalating resentment, hostility, and outrage are never resolved because the period at the end of that sentence stops the communication. You believe this situation is a done deal with no further discussion or alternative outcome. Your anger burns at an indifferent, inconsistent, and inactive God. However, there is an immeasurable difference when you insert a comma and the words "but I trust You" at the end of that sentence. "God! God! I don't understand, *but I trust You*" allows the Almighty the ability to respond as you give Him the responsibility to fix it. Even if your world is turned upside down, you can trust that God knows and is on it. Chaos might be happening, but you can trust God with the circumstance.

Jesus likewise calls you to Him. You are to bring your battered soul, broken heart, and busted dreams to Him.

> Come to me, all you who are weary and burdened, and I will give you rest. Take my yoke upon you and learn from me, for I am gentle and humble in heart,

and you will find rest for your souls. For my yoke is
easy and my burden is light. (Matthew 11:28–30)

Picture yourself running to the arms of Jesus. Take your fatigue, brokenness, and confusion to Jesus, ready for Him to mend whatever is fractured and soothe whatever is agitated.

Can you see yourself collapsing in Jesus's arms and Him healing your wounded soul?

The Focus of Faith

I would imagine that you, like me, need a visual connection in a relationship. We need to be face-to-face with those to whom we are communicating—thank goodness for Skype, Zoom, and FaceTime when the pandemic made it impossible to coexist in a room together! At the very least, we need to hear someone's voice to experience the dynamics of a relationship.

We tend to think of God as invisible. Trusting in something we cannot see, touch, or hear is unnatural. How can you even communicate with someone like that? My friend, God is anything but invisible! We see God's hand in all things. The consistent order of days and nights. The miracle of conception and birth. The breathtaking beauty of sunrises and sunsets. The power of lightning and the deafening roar of thunderstorms. The awe of inexplicable miracles.

Romans 1:20 warns, "Since the creation of the world God's invisible qualities—his eternal power and divine nature—have been clearly seen, being understood from what has been made, so that men are without excuse."

Scripture boldly states that the splendor of nature and all of God's glorious creation reveal the existence and power of God, so no one has any excuse for not honoring or acknowledging Him.

Faith crushes any doubt that God is who He says He is. Faith acknowledges the splendor, holiness, and perfection of God. Faith provides the confidence that God will deliver despite the circumstances that are waging war with your mind, body, and spirit. Faith is a form of worshipping God because you trust Him. Hebrews 11:6 says, "Without faith it is impossible to please God, because anyone who comes to him must believe that he exists and that he rewards those who earnestly seek him." Faith must have an object, and the proper object of genuine faith is God.

Hebrews 11 chronicles men and women of faith in the Bible who followed God's Word even when it related to things that had not yet occurred. They obeyed God out of complete trust in His promises. The world had never seen rain when God commanded Noah to build that massive ark.

Hebrews 11:7 says, "By faith Noah, when warned about things not yet seen ... built an ark to save his family." Can you imagine the ridicule Noah received for 120 years as he constructed that vessel to God's specific measurements in a parched, landlocked area? It was unthinkable there could ever be enough water to float that boat!

People during Noah's time lived to be an average of 900 years old, so time was calculated differently than now. Noah was 600 years old when he began construction on the ark, and he died at age 950. But 120 years was still a sizable chunk of Noah's remaining life that was dedicated to fulfilling God's request to build the ark, especially when rain had never fallen. Noah knew that the One who mandated this construction was worthy to be trusted and followed. And you know the end of the story works out well for Noah and his family and all that mixture of critters inside the ark. Noah's faithful obedience to God's directive saved their lives and got the world jump-started again. Persevering by trusting and pursuing God's Word is your lifeline on this side of heaven.

Do you have faith? In what or whom do you put it?

Loosen Your Grip

You mustn't hold on to this world. Your life span, even if you live for one hundred years, is but a teeny speck on the timeline of eternity. Scripture concurs. James 4:14 says, "What is your life? You are a mist that appears for a little while and then vanishes." That is not real encouraging. I don't think of mists as having staying power! But in God's economy, the significance is not on this side of heaven but on the other side. Eternity is a really, really long time. It has no end. It just keeps on going. So ask yourself, where do you want to put your focus?

Second Corinthians 4:18 reminds us, "So we fix our eyes not on what is seen, but on what is unseen. For what is seen is temporary, but what is unseen is eternal."

Dear one, your focus needs to be on what is eternal, what is lasting … forever. While the unseen realities may be invisible, they are no less real. Eternity is enduring, indestructible, and permanent, whereas all earthly things are perishable and waste away in time. Do not falter in seeking God's face first rather than being wooed by the temporary prizes, possessions, or positions of this present world. Yes, there is beauty, joy, and satisfaction in relationships, successes, and the cherished moments of life. That is all good. But God should be your first love.

How do you keep yourself from being impacted by the temptations of the world?

Sin Messed Everything Up!

Unfortunately, you and I possess a very unsavory characteristic called sin. It is a mean, nasty, and dark trait rooted in our hearts and expressed through our thoughts, words, and actions. And it can really hurt people—even the people we love the most.

But we are not alone. Everyone who breathes is a sinner. Romans 3:23 pronounces this guilty verdict: "For all have sinned and fall short of the glory of God."

OK. It gets worse. Romans 8:7–8 continues this theme: "The sinful mind is hostile to God. It does not submit to God's law, nor can it do so. Those controlled by the sinful nature cannot please God."

In other words, as sinful people, we are not capable of upholding God's standard of living. We yield to our own selfish desires and oppose obedience and full surrender to God's statutes. That insubordination to God's righteous requirements is unacceptable to Him.

God reveals what is most displeasing in Proverbs 6:16–19: "There are six things the Lord hates, seven that are detestable to him: haughty eyes, a lying tongue, hands that shed innocent blood, a heart that devises wicked schemes, feet that are quick to rush into evil, a false witness who pours out lies and a man who stirs up dissension among brothers."

These loathsome qualities destroy relationships. The first casualty of Adam and Eve's transgression of eating the forbidden fruit in the garden was a broken relationship with God. Your Father cherishes His relationships with His children. When your heart is darkened with sin, you just cannot, on your own, fix the problem to comply with the standards of a holy and perfect God.

Romans 3:10–18 speaks to the power of sin universally and how it corrupts humanity.

Below is a sampling of verses that describe our condition:
- There is no one righteous, not even one (v. 10).
- No one who seeks God (v. 11).
- All have turned away (v. 12).
- They have together become worthless (v. 12).
- Their tongues practice deceit (v. 13).

- Ruin and misery mark their ways (v. 16).
- And the way of peace they do not know (v. 17).
- There is no fear of God before their eyes (v. 18).

Those are some strong words that speak of the restless and twisted nature of our hearts with no inclination to honor God. We are prone to wander, drifting from embracing God while getting distracted by the temptations of this world and our own flesh. As Romans 7:19 articulates, "For what I do is not the good I want to do; no, the evil I do not want to do—this I keep on doing." A fitting picture of the power of sin.

And then the dagger! Romans 6:23 says: "For the wages of sin is death." An undisciplined carnal life that lives for the gratification of self rather than living for the affections of God is given over to sin and will result in spiritual death. In other words, sin produces a separation from God for eternity. Unfortunately, this scenario describes all humanity. Sin occupies all our lives and creates a very bleak eternal future.

That is the bad news. Here is the good news: God had a plan to remedy this dismal situation.

He loves you that much!

God's Costly Rescue Plan

You and I could never earn our way into heaven based on our own merits. Our filthy sins would never grant us entry into heaven when we die. To be able to enter heaven on good works means we would have to be faultless because God is perfect, righteous, and unchangeable. Heaven is a holy place. God knows that even despite our good intentions and compassionate actions, humanity is inclined toward corrupt motives and selfish ambitions. God knows people are broken and wayward. He knows every person who breathes and populates the world has a less than perfect track record with failures and flaws. That includes you and me. This truth presents God with a serious dilemma. He loves us dearly, but as a just God, He cannot let our sins go unpunished and cannot let us enter heaven based on our talented but tainted actions.

God's plan for the salvation of fallen humanity came with an exorbitant price—the sacrifice of His only Son, Jesus Christ. Jesus, the Son of God, was perfect. Holy. Sinless. Innocent of any wrongdoing.

William is my only son, and I could not and would not willfully sacrifice him for anyone. Yet our loving Father in heaven did that very thing, as we read in John 3:16: "For God so loved the world that he gave his one and only Son, that whoever believes in him shall not perish but have eternal life." God's love for all people is what motivated His plan to save the world for eternity through the death of His Son, Jesus Christ.

In obedience to God's plan of salvation, Jesus intentionally bore the crushing weight of the sins of guilty humankind and the heavy burden of our depravity in His death on the cross. He was crucified to appease and absorb His Father's wrath against humanity's corrupt nature.

God's rescue plan provided that the sins of humankind were transferred to Jesus on the cross and that, in return, fallen humanity was granted and credited with the righteousness and holiness of Jesus. In this exchange, we deserved God's harsh judgment for our selfish, wanton, and prideful pursuits, but instead, we received the forgiveness and blamelessness of Jesus through His death as though we had never sinned. Jesus, in full obedience to His Father, endured the horrific torture and cruelty of the crucifixion as He received God's full fury for the sins of humanity hurled at Himself. Jesus's sacrifice allows us to spend eternity in the hallowedness of heaven.

A Free Gift

Sin and death were conquered at the cross! God's intervention in human history through Jesus's sacrifice displays the abundance of His glory, goodness, and grace. In His plan of salvation, God's grace gave us what we did not deserve—eternal life with Him when we breathe our last breath on this side of heaven.

Ephesians 2:8–9 says, "For it is by grace you have been saved, through faith—and this not from yourselves, it is the gift of God—not by works, so that no one can boast."

Recognizing yourself as a sinner, understanding you can do nothing to earn your way into heaven, and surrendering yourself by placing your faith in Jesus Christ alone as your Lord and Savior assures eternal life with Him forever rather than being eternally separated from Him at death. Good people don't get into heaven; forgiven people do.

This free gift of eternal life through God's abundant grace is offered to all. As in any gift, it must be received and opened to enjoy the blessings within rather than remain unopened and unused.

When you first place your belief in Jesus, the Holy Spirit enters your heart, lavishly and continually pouring out His love on you as He permanently dwells there. The Holy Spirit is God's advocate and helper in your new life as a believer. He reveals God's thoughts and teachings, intercedes for you in times of weakness, and guides you to live in truth and Christlike wisdom. Oh, what a glorious gift we receive by grace through faith to be the heirs of God's rich inheritance for eternity! What thankfulness in our hearts we have to God for loving us so large!

The only One who can affect your eternal destination is God. His restoration plan sets you apart as holy and purified in His eyes through your faith in His Son, Jesus Christ. Jesus, your loving Savior, would rather die than live without you for eternity. He is so worthy of your worship!

Jesus said, "I am the light of the world. Whoever follows me will never walk in darkness, but will have the light of life" (John 8:12).

Do you want the light of Jesus to be reflected in your life? Will you follow Him?

Scars as Beauty Marks!

Scars reveal your personal stories and battles. Some would say the more gnarled and deeper the scar, the better!

I wonder … when God calls us Home and we are face-to-face with Jesus, will He show us His scars? Will we see the places where the deep spikes were hammered into His hands and feet as He was nailed to the cross? Or the deep gashes on His back from the brutal whipping He endured during his mock trial before His crucifixion? Oh, how those scars indicate His love for you and me—a love that can never be separated! How Jesus proved His devotion to humankind through the gruesome ordeal that produced those deep wounds.

The questions I pose on this side of heaven are these: Will you be able to show sweet Jesus the scars that you have endured for Him? Have you repented of behaviors not honorable to God and that you know need to be changed or even fully jettisoned from your life? Have those changes, once made, alienated your friends or close comrades who still operate from that old combat zone that you have just vacated? Have you faced conflict, ridicule, or rejection because of your faith? Are you continuing to grow in your faith, or are you cutting back in fear of offending others? Do you reach outside your comfort zone to serve those different from you or to love the unlovable? To help those who are in great need and who require your energy, time, and capacity, which are already in short supply in your life at this moment? May Jesus's words in John 15:8 reflect how you abide in Christ and radiate Him for all to see: "This is to my Father's glory, that you bear much fruit, showing yourself to be my disciples."

How delighted our Savior will be to see your sacrificial scars! To know that they represent exhaustion, pain, and surrender in His name. They might have distanced the affections of some people close to you or caused you discomfort and inconvenience, but ultimately, they will create a plentiful, fruit-bearing harvest through you that produces a greater abundance for others. How God is glorified as you follow and serve His Son. My friend, Jesus will see those scars as beauty marks!

Share Your Wounds!

Our lives are messy. Once you leave your mother's womb, conflict, sin, and adversity stand ready to welcome you into this new adventure called life. And yes, life can be hard. In the course of time, perhaps you have made decisions that have not gone well for you. Perhaps you have allowed pride, greed, and deception to hurt, or even ruin, the relationships dearest to you. Maybe you have let undisciplined behavior corrupt your life rather than serve the needs of others. Through it all, perhaps you have competed for the praise and adoration of the world rather than played for an audience of One.

And then you met Jesus. You realize that this new relationship is a game changer in the way you think and act. That the standard of living He calls you to follow is for your protection and provision. It means listening to others rather than positioning yourself to be heard. It means serving others rather than seeking to be served. It means exhibiting self-control and kindness rather than abusive and harmful behavior. It reminds you that words can be destructive weapons, so guard your tongue.

As you settle into this new relationship with Jesus, do the unthinkable—share your wounds! Be honest. Be authentic. Be real. People will relate to your former ways. They will see themselves in similar unruly situations. Do not hide these wounds out of shame, embarrassment, or pride, but be open and vulnerable with others to let them know how you are now walking in freedom rather than being held hostage by your prior sinful pursuits that once exerted control over your life. Share with others that Jesus is the source of your new strength, joy, and perspective. He has uprooted you from situations that were far from favorable and, in some instances, has rescued you from very dark places. He has given you a peace that passes all understanding—no matter the circumstance. You are walking in victorious transformation because of new purpose and hope.

Let people know the impact Jesus has had on your life. You are now experiencing wholeness because you have ditched, dumped, and discarded behaviors that were damaging to healthy living and loving relationships. There is freedom in the healing that only Jesus can provide. Share your wounds with others so they can see the restoration that comes from loving and trusting Christ.

The outrageous grace of God reaches out to a lost and rebellious world. The wounds you once had, so deeply carved into your body, mind, and soul, are now replaced by the immeasurable love and relentless redemption of Jesus.

May we be walking, breathing, and serving people whose lives glorify God. May we think, act, and communicate in ways that highly prioritize eternal consequences rather than just the tyranny of the urgent. May we be the visible image of the invisible God. May that be accomplished as we wear Jesus well and share with others the healing that only He can provide. It is a healing that transforms our tattered lives and damaged relationships into joyful hope and flourishing days!

Are you willing to share your wounds?

Hope Unleashed

Hope is a *powerful* word.

Hope is what propels people to sacrifice for a better life, for a noble cause, or for a devoted relationship. Hope restores joy when life throws curveballs. Hope ignites faith when your brokenness seems too difficult to endure, your prognosis seems too grim to bear, or your suffering seems too painful to withstand. Hope rescues you when your world is rocked to its core and when your life is stuck on hold. When you are in a bad place.

Hope is ushered in through the person of Jesus Christ. He is the Son of God and God incarnate. He is a holy, perfect, righteous, and innocent man whose mission was to die, out of obedience to His Father, for your guilty transgressions and mine, so we could spend eternity in heaven. God, rich in grace, mercy, and love for you, sacrificed Jesus so you could be saved through faith in His Son. Jesus fulfilled God's promise of eternal life for those who believe. *Confidence in God's revealed eternal future provides an assurance of hope.*

Hope is a *joyful* word.

Romans 12:12 encourages you to be joyful in hope. Psalm 42:5 says to put your hope in God. All biblical hope comes from God. He is faithful, despite your past or current circumstances. God delivers on His promises, so your hope is cheerful confidence that His goodness will be accomplished in the future. You have the blessed assurance you can count on excellent things from the King of glory. You believe with certainty He has a plan and a purpose for you that will shower His favor on you. God loves you, delights in you, and never forsakes you. What joy! Hope propels that joy.

Hope is an *action* word.

Hope is not meant to be hidden or silenced. Life is a war zone. Lives are at stake on this bloodied spiritual battlefield every moment. Hope is meant to infiltrate, not insulate. To fight in the trenches. To lead the charge. Hope must crusade for the lives and souls of those dealing with difficult issues in this fallen, dark, and damaged world. It must resurrect a collapsed society. It must repair broken people, mend fractured families, and ignite chilled relationships. God is recruiting you on this battlefront to help people break free from the bondage that entangles them and experience the grace and regenerating power of Jesus Christ. Or perhaps you are in a grueling season of life and need that high-octane hope in your empty spiritual, emotional, mental, and physical fuel tank.

My friend, you are not alone. Lay your struggles, fatigue, and sorrows at God's throne of grace. You can be assured that He hears, sees, knows, and cares. Trusting in Him will provide you with hope … no matter the circumstances.

> May the God of hope fill you with all joy and peace as you trust in him, so that you may overflow with hope by the power of the Holy Spirit. (Romans 15:13)

Eternal Destination

Bob had his first cancer surgery, and it was a doozy. Intensive care for a few days followed by a week in the hospital. William was six. As I was bathing him the first night after Bob's surgery, William asked, "Mommy, is Daddy going to die?" My heart skipped a beat. Totally caught off guard, my reply was, "He doesn't intend to, sweetheart." I knew that answer wasn't good enough. The next day at the hospital, I shared William's important question with Bob and asked my beloved hunk of a husband to think about how he would respond. Then I prayed William would not ask that question again until Bob came home from the hospital.

By God's grace, William waited until Bob came home, and as the three of us were together, he looked straight at Bob and asked, "Daddy, are you going to die?"

Bob's response was not only epic but further spoke the Gospel to our little boy.

"Yes, William. Daddy is going to die." Then looking directly at me, Bob said, "And, William, Mommy is going to die someday too." Then looking intently at William, Bob said softly, "And, William, someday—and I hope it is a long time from now—you are going to die. So, William, the question is not if Daddy is going to die but where will I go after I die?"

To which William, our little theologian who did not miss a beat, enthusiastically replied, "Oh, Daddy! Daddy! You will be in heaven with Jesus! You will not feel any more pain! Oh, Daddy! That will be a good thing to be in heaven with Jesus someday!"

William never again asked his daddy if he was going to die.

> Let the word of Christ dwell in you richly as you teach and admonish one another with all wisdom, and as you sing psalms, hymns, and spiritual songs with gratitude in your hearts to God. And whatever you do, whether in word or deed, do it all in the name of the Lord Jesus, giving thanks to God the Father through him. (Colossians 3:16–17)

Final Questions

And so, dear friend, I ask: If you were to die tonight, what would be your eternal destination?

Your choices are limited. The Bible gives us two options: heaven or hell. The requirements for entry into heaven are strict: being perfect and righteous. Only one person in the history of the world made that cut on His own perfect merits. Not any of the Old Testament prophets. Not Mother Teresa. Not Billy Graham. Only Jesus. The Son of God. Holy. Sinless. Blameless. Humankind's wretched sin disqualifies anyone from immediate entry into heaven on their own performance, worth, or goodness. Jesus intentionally died for you so that you could spend eternity with Him. That was God's restoration plan—His tender mercy of not giving you what you truly deserve and His outrageous grace of giving you what you don't deserve. This gift from God offers the unobtainable entry into heaven to every person who puts their faith in Jesus Christ as Lord and Savior.

Nothing in your past prevents you from receiving God's grace. All sins are level at the foot of the cross. Hanging on that cross with Jesus centuries ago were the sins of broken humanity … past, present, and future. Jesus took them, claimed them, and forgave them. He then passed on His gift of righteousness to you that allows you to enter the gates of heaven. However, like any gift, you must receive it. You can't leave it unopened, or it won't reveal its treasures.

So it begs the second question: Have you received the gift of eternal life by accepting Jesus Christ as your Lord and Savior? If not, now is the perfect time! You are not promised tomorrow. Please consider the eternal consequences. To receive this gift of salvation that God offers you, please pray this simple prayer: "Lord Jesus, I confess that I am a sinner, and I ask forgiveness. There is nothing I can do to earn my way into heaven. I believe You died for my sins. I surrender my life to You and place my faith in You as my Lord and Savior. Thank You for Your sacrifice, Your forgiveness of my sins, and Your assurance of this gift of eternal life. It is in Your name, the name of Jesus, I pray. Amen."

This gift received is a game changer! Joy, freedom, and peace will embrace you. Yes, you will still sin. Yes, you will still think, say, and do things contrary to God's best for you. The enemy will be after you with full fury. Repenting and confessing your sins daily will continue to restore the communion between you and God that is compromised through unrighteous living. However, He loves you with an everlasting, unconditional love and will never forsake you. Truly, you are His cherished child, and He is your beloved Father even when you stray.

Please find a church where you can be part of a supportive community. Start reading the Bible, which is the inerrant Word of God. The book of

John in the New Testament is the best starting place in the Bible. Following the standards set forth in the Bible, God's standards, will help you master the skill of living. Read a proverb a day and a psalm a day. There are also many daily devotionals in Christian bookstores and online to strengthen your heart with God's Word and to protect your soul against the raging battles of this world and the temptations of the enemy that are aggressively competing for your allegiance. Journal your feelings and thoughts using the applications in *Restored* that pertain to you.

God's infinite graciousness and kindness abound in His forgiveness. "If we confess our sins, he is faithful and just and will forgive us our sins and purify us from all unrighteousness" (1 John 1:9).

The enemy has no authority over God's kids. Remember, as a believer, you are a child of the King. You have a royal inheritance. Thankfully, the end of the story does not go well for the devil, but it will be glorious for you!

If you have already made that decision to let Jesus Christ reign as your Lord and Savior, continue to treasure that magnificent relationship with Him. Encourage others to encounter the everlasting love found in Christ. Life is hard, and traveling this journey without Him would be like trying to drive to Seattle from Miami without a road map, GPS, and cell phone. Throw in a broken gas gauge, windshield wipers that don't work, and no spare tire. That would sum up my sense of loss if Jesus was not in the driver's seat.

You were born and then will have a number of unknown days until you breathe your final breath. What matters is what you do with the dash between your birth and death years. You don't know how many days that dash represents, but make it count for eternal purposes rather than feverishly collecting earthly treasures that will not last. Loving well, forgiving, encouraging, persevering, praying, showing grace and mercy, acting justly, being compassionate, forgiving some more, walking in humility, and serving others are all forms of worship that glorify God and point to Him. People are watching how you respond when you are soaring from the mountaintops but particularly when you are scorched in the desert. Show them you choose joy no matter the circumstances. Show them your hope is in Jesus even when you can't see the finish line. He will lead you there ... or carry you over it!

God beckons! It is the most beautiful story ever told—the story of God's restoration plan. The story of God reconnecting all of life's broken pieces so that you and I can experience full joy, indescribable hope, and immeasurable love on this side of heaven and then in heaven itself. Isn't that just like Him? To God be the glory!

I pray that you, being rooted and established in love,
may have power, together with all the saints,
to grasp how wide and long and high and deep
is the love of Christ, and to know this love that surpasses
knowledge—that you may be filled to the measure
of all the fullness of God.

(Ephesians 3:17–19)

ACKNOWLEDGMENTS

Writing a book is a long journey with derailments and distractions along the way. It is a constant war with words to express the depth of the heart and the significance of each victory and defeat. I wrote this book over seven years with the investment of so many people praying, cheering, and encouraging me to cross the finish line.

Brenda, you have been the one person who has shared all but twenty months of my life, and that is only because I am your older sister by that many months. Mom and Dad inspired us with the beauty of their resilience, perseverance, and courage. Oh, how they mastered the skill of living! The heartbreak we endured through Mom's loss was the same, but the journey we have traveled since then has been uniquely our own. You are my greatest advocate and best friend. I appreciate what you have taught me and the sound counsel you have given on issues that matter. May these pages be an encouragement to you and to my cherished Connor and Connolly. I love you so much!

I owe such thankfulness to Barb Peil, who has walked with me, coached me, and helped edit *Restored*'s manuscript. She taught me not to waste words. Barb bolstered my confidence every step of the way. I treasured my multiple trips to her home in Colorado and later in California, where we would have great fun-filled adventures and do a little work on my book at the same time! God bless you, beloved Barb, as my cherished sister in Christ.

Carol Johnson is my treasured and talented executive assistant who has been my life manager for the past twelve years. She would remind me when I was letting distractions get in the way of completing the book. Carol provided her keen, critical eye and wisdom to multiple passages that needed clarification. Couldn't have completed *Restored* without my dear Carol! Additionally, a special word of gratitude to Carol's handsome and supportive husband, Butch, who helped with the book's technology demands that needed attention.

Katina, your brother was the love of my life. We were best friends and married for fifteen years. Bob shaped my thinking, influenced my behavior, and awed me with his deep faith and strength of character. There is not a day that goes by that I don't think of the man I adored who forever captured my heart. Katina, many thanks for your prayers for *Restored* and for being a beautiful and cherished part of Bob's, William's, and my life.

Oh, the power of prayer! So many endearing friends have prayed for this book *for years*! Betty Lovell, Connie Yates, Jackie Thornton, and Mary Dowling are my Fave Five sisters. We have known each other for over thirty-five years through our work with courageous pediatric cancer patients. This sweet friendship began through Wipe Out Kids' Cancer, a nonprofit organization I founded in 1980 in memory of Mom. (Wipe Out Kids' Cancer will receive half the net proceeds from *Restored*.) The Fave Five sisters are devoted to one another, and their prayers have undergirded *Restored* for years. My life has been enriched by this deep and precious sisterhood.

Jo Tiller, Lynn McDonough, and Vicki Hitzges are my Seeker Sisters. We meet weekly at my home for Bible study, fellowship, and prayer as part of Watermark Community Church in Dallas. They have prayed me through *Restored* and challenged me when I was letting interruptions get in the way. Such a joy doing life with Jo, Lynn, and Vicki! Please don't call me on Wednesday nights; I am doing "community" with the three of them!

Meg Adams has been my prayer warrior for thirty-five years. I have watched her and Steve raise three wonderful children—Grace, Heather, and

Kyle—who are now married, and some have children of their own. It has been a privilege to be very involved in their lives and feel the power of their prayers envelop this book.

My dear "Barnabas," Dianne Ogle, has been a faithful source of encouragement to me for multiple decades. Her prayers, counsel, letters, and texts have inspired me and propelled me forward. I call her my Barnabas, and she calls me her Paul—the two leaders worked together in the life and ministry of the early church. Dianne's talents, strategic thinking, and intercessory prayer have empowered me throughout this entire literary project.

Many thanks to Suzanne and Tim Schutze for standing with me for forty years. Their beautiful Grace is my goddaughter. The Schutzes are cherished by me and have blessed me with their abiding friendship.

Stan Levenson is my mentor. His profound intelligence, kindness, and talents have impacted me both personally and professionally. We were business partners in the public relations arena for many years before he retired. Stan is a role model to multiple generations of people. He is simply Stantastic! How I treasure both Stan and his amazing wife, Barbara!

Mike and Martha Howard were my comrades and best friends three days every week for over a year when I went to our family ranch to write. The ranch is hallowed ground, and the quietness, even with the coyotes howling at night, inspired my creativity. My early-morning drives to Starbucks with Mike riding shotgun started my long days of writing with caffeine and beautiful fellowship. I always knew Mike and Martha were praying for me throughout the day as I was poring over my manuscript. Such is their love and commitment to me over the forty years Mike has managed the ranch, and the Howards have been part of our family.

To Doug Wood, how I appreciated your encouraging texts, clever words of wisdom, and creative poems. Your support prompted me to move forward with confidence. You are so special to William and me!

To Susan and Don Riley, Paula and Bob Strasser, Mary and Mike Poss, Karee and Greg Sampson, Patrice and Dave Peterson, Karen and Steve Morriss, Aislinn and Sam Blankenship, Lydia and LaMontry Lott, Dee and Billy Howell, Julie and Todd Doshier, Carol Weyman, Lesli Lehman, and Janet Beaver, I am so thankful for your love and prayers for me to finish strong. They have now been answered. I praise God for you!

Christina, Eric, and Mark, I love you. May *Restored* encourage and strengthen you in this beautiful and crazy thing called life.

To Athena Dean Holtz, Carol Tetzlaff, Sara Cormany, and the talented team at Redemption Press, many thanks for helping me get this book into the hands of those who will benefit from it. Your encouragement, experience, and excellence every step of the way kept me moving forward. Many thanks for shepherding me in the process.

I am profoundly appreciative of my esteemed endorsers. They are friends I greatly admire. Whether celebrated in sports, ministry, media, education, entertainment, business, or social culture, they have carved a stellar reputation as key opinion leaders in their arenas of expertise and are outstanding human beings. I am grateful beyond measure for their encouraging and touching words about *Restored* and their delight in the book.

Dear friend, many thanks for choosing to engage in *Restored*. My prayer is that this is more than a book for you. May it be a lasting roadmap to provide hope and joy on this wonderful, messy, fun, and challenging journey called life. It is an honor to share my story with you and to encourage you as you pursue yours. May you persevere, treasure your relationships, and choose joy daily as you move forward. Onward you go!

Family matters. My mother and father are not living, but their impact will forever be alive in me. Mom's passing began my journey of faith that is chronicled early in *Restored*. I was twelve when this cataclysmic event of her death crushed my family. But the determination, courage, kindness, and humility my parents fully displayed and lavishly showered on Brenda and me shaped my thinking and actions. Yes, their DNA is mine, but more importantly, their examples of goodness, devotion, and truth are what spoke to my soul. I was so blessed with their deep love and their encouragement to always pursue my dreams.

Bob was my soulmate. His story of faith, bravery, and compassion forever inspires me and boldly speaks within the pages of this book. Bob and I had planned to write our story together when he recovered from his illness, but that improvement never happened. *Restored* had to wait until William, nine at the time of his daddy's passing, graduated from high school and was in college. Cancer may have claimed Bob's life, but his legacy lives robustly within these chapters and within our hearts. He will always be our hero.

Finally, dear William, you are my greatest joy. You are just like your extraordinary father in word, looks, and deed! You inspired us both with your maturity at such a young age dealing with his illness and passing. Now, years later, you carry on his legacy of faith, strength, and courage with such joy, dignity, and confidence. I rejoice that you are our beloved son!

In closing, I give heartfelt thanks and joyful praise to my Lord and Savior, Jesus Christ. He is so worthy of our worship! To God be the glory!

ENDNOTES

1   Beth Moore, "These Words of Mine," Part 2, Sermons.love, https://sermons.love/beth-moore/13662-beth-moore-these-words-of-mine-part-2.html.

2   Lao Tzu, *Tao Te Ching*, 400 BC.

3   Rosa Parks, "On the Possibility of Arrest," from "Civil Rights Icon Rosa Parks Dies," radio interview with Lynn Neary, NPR, October 25, 2005, https://www.npr.org/2005/10/25/4973548/civil-rights-icon-rosa-parks-dies.

4   Wayne Jackson, "All Things Work Together for Good: Controversy or Comfort?" ChristianCourier.com.

5   Ann Voskamp, *The Way of Abundance: A 60-Day Journey into a Deeply Meaningful Life* (Nashville, TN: Thomas Nelson, 2018).

6   Maureen Connolly, *Forehand Drive* (London: Maggibbon and Kee, 1957).

7   C. S. Lewis, *The Screwtape Letters* (New York: Macmillan, 1980), 132.

8   Joni Eareckson Tada, *Hope ... The Best of Things* (Wheaton, IL: Crossway Books, 2007).

9   G. K. Chesterton, *The Innocence of Father Brown* (New Kensington, PA: Whitaker House, 2013).

10 Connie Pryzant, "Up from Tragedy," *Dallas Morning News,* March 9, 1986.

11 Pryzant, "Up from Tragedy."

12 Robert J. Morgan, *The Red Sea Rules: 10 God-Given Strategies for Difficult Times* (Nashville, TN: Thomas Nelson, 2014).

13 Horatio Gates Spafford, "When Peace, Like a River," 1873.

14 Oscar Wilde, "The Portrait of Mr. W. H" short story (New York: HarperPerennial Classics, 2014).

15 Vince Lombardi Jr., *What It Takes to Be #1: Vince Lombardi on*

Leadership (New York: McGraw Hill, 2003).

16   C. S. Lewis, *The Four Loves* (New York: Harper Collins, 1960).

17   Bob Curley, "More Americans Are Binge Drinking During Pandemic: How to Cope Without Alcohol," Healthline, https://www.healthline.com/health-news/more-americans-are-binge-drinking-during-pandemic-how-to-cope-without-alcohol, October 5, 2020.

18   National Center for Health Statistics, "Early Release of Selected Mental Health Estimates," Centers for Disease Control, released May 2020, https://www.cdc.gov/nchs/data/nhis/earlyrelease/ERmentalhealth-508.pdf.

19   National Center for Health Statistics, "Early Release."

20   Anjel Vahratian, Stephen J. Blumberg, Emily P. Terlizzi, and Jeannine S. Schiller, "Symptoms of Anxiety or Depressive Disorder and Use of Mental Health Care Among Adults During the COVID-19 Pandemic—United States, August 2020–February 2021," *Morbidity and Mortality Weekly Report* 70, no. 13 (April 2, 2021): 490–494.

21   Carol Kent, *When I Lay My Isaac Down* (Colorado Springs, CO: NavPress, 2004).

22   Maureen Connolly Brinker, monthly column in *Tennis* magazine, reprinted in *The Best of Brinker* by the Maureen Connolly Brinker Tennis Foundation.

23   Cahleen Shrier, PhD, "The Science of the Crucifixion," Azusa Pacific University, March 1, 2002.

24   Corrie ten Boom, "Corrie ten Boom on Forgiveness" from November 1972, *Guideposts Classics*, July 24, 2014.

25   Beth Moore, *Seeking a Heart Like His* (Nashville, TN: Lifeway, 2010).

26   Corrie ten Boom, *Guideposts Classics.*

27   John Piper, "When Words Are Wind," Desiring God, November 10, 1993, https://www.desiringgod.org/articles/when-words-are-wind.

28   Nuraly S. Akimbekov and Mohammed S. Razzaque, "Laughter therapy: A Humor-Induced Hormonal Intervention to Reduce Stress and Anxiety," National Library of Medicine, https://pubmed.ncbi.nlm.nih.gov/34642668/.

29   Mary Payne Bennett, Cecile Lengacher, "Humor and Laughter May Influence Health IV. Humor and Immune Function," National Library of Medicine, https://pubmed.ncbi.nlm.nih.gov/18955287/.

30   Tri-City Medical Center, "5 Ways the Sun Impacts Your Mental and Physical Health," https://www.tricitymed.org/2018/08/5-ways-the-sun-impacts-your-mental-and-physical-health/.

31   Tim Elmore, "Six Fears and Concerns of College Students Today," Growing Leaders, www.growingleaders.com/tim-elmore/, accessed May 31, 2012.

32   Oscar Wilde, Jules Barbey d'Aurevilly, Lady Wilde, *The Writings of Oscar Wilde* (A. R. Keller & Company, Incorporated, 1907), 113.

33   Rick Renner, "Can God Entrust You with More?," *Monthly Teaching Letter*, May 26, 2015.

34   Ailsa Harvey and Elizabeth Howell, "How Many Galaxies Are There?," February 1, 2022, https://www.space.com/25303-how-many-galaxies-are-in-the-universe.html.

ORDER INFORMATION

REDEMPTION
P R E S S

To order additional copies of this book, please visit
www.redemption-press.com.
Also available at Christian bookstores, Amazon, and Barnes and Noble.